ARIANA

ARIANA

The Unauthorized Biography

DANNY WHITE

MICHAEL O'MARA

ARIANA

The Unauthorized Biography

DANNY WHITE

MICHAEL O'MARA BOOKS

First published in Great Britain in 2017 by
Michael O'Mara Books Limited
9 Lion Yard
Tremadoc Road
London SW4 7NQ

A CIP catalogue record for this book is available from the British
Library.

Papers used by Michael O'Mara Books Limited are natural, recyclable
products made from wood grown in sustainable forests. The
manufacturing processes conform to the environmental regulations
of the country of origin.

ISBN: 978-1-78243-885-4 in hardback print format
ISBN: 978-1-78243-886-1 in ebook format

1 2 3 4 5 6 7 8 9 10

Designed and typeset by D23

Printed and bound by CPI Group (UK) Ltd, Croydon, CR0 4YY

CONTENTS

Introduction   7

Chapter One • THE EARLY YEARS   11

Chapter Two • A FLAIR FOR THE THEATRE   27

Chapter Three • HER FIRST BIG BREAK   43

Chapter Four • A CHANGE OF FAITH   67

Chapter Five • A MUSICAL DEBUT   77

Chapter Six • THE 'DIFFICULT SECOND ALBUM'   107

Chapter Seven • STORMY SEAS   129

Chapter Eight • #donutgate   151

Chapter Nine • THIRD TIME'S THE CHARM   161

Chapter Ten • TRAGEDY AND TERROR   183

Chapter Eleven • FROM THE ASHES   193

Chapter Twelve • LOOKING TO THE FUTURE   205

Discography   211

Awards   213

Bibliography   214

Picture Credits   215

Index   217

INTRODUCTION

The sun was shining but events in the closing weeks of spring in 2017 shrouded Britain in darkness. There was no darker moment than the one in which a young man attacked Ariana Grande's Manchester concert, killing twenty-two people and injuring 250. Within days of the bombing, Ariana announced that she would stage a benefit concert back in Manchester. Preparations began for an event that it was hoped would heal the wounds of a nation.

Then, the evening before the concert to be staged at the Old Trafford cricket ground, terrorists struck once again, this time in London.

Yet Grande, the small girl with a big name, would not be cowed. She pressed ahead with the concert. Some 50,000 people attended the show, where the likes of Justin Bieber, Katy Perry, Take That and Liam Gallagher performed. Then, Ariana took to the stage. Her set was to be the climax of the show, and the pinnacle of her set was her rendition of the classic show tune 'Over the Rainbow'.

Ariana looked so small on the stage, which stretched in front of the vast audience. She sung the song beautifully, despite the almost throttling emotion of the moment. Yet near its end, her emotions bubbled over and she stood holding a hand to her face, her famous hair caught up in her fingers. In the audience, too, feelings began to run higher than ever as fans, some of whom had been at the fateful first concert, broke down in tears. The musicians stopped playing as Ariana composed herself and the audience roared its encouragement. Then she began to sing again, nailing the song's big climax and blowing a kiss to the audience. Despite her small stature – she stands at a little over five feet tall – she had been a giant on the night. There is a concept in Kabbalah, Ariana's spiritual belief system, known as *tikkun olam*. It means an act that helps put back together the shattered parts of the universe. Ariana had performed a model act of *tikkun olam* and become a global hero.

Or, as a writer for the respected and sombre business news website *Bloomberg* put it: Ariana was 'the leader of the free world for a day'.

'Over the Rainbow', which connects with people's hopes and dreams and their yearning for a place where the troubles of the world magically disappear, was a fine choice for the big moment – and it held extra significance for Ariana. As a child, she loved the music of Judy Garland, who originally sang it in the movie of *The Wizard of Oz*. Ariana also appeared in a stage production of *Oz* as a kid in Florida, so to sing it on the biggest stage, to a global audience, made the choice of song all the more significant.

Those productions came as a welcome distraction for her, an escape from a sometimes testing childhood. Yet even as she trod the boards of the local youth theatre, she could never have imagined that she would eventually sing Garland's big ballad in such charged circumstances. When the moment came, the whole world was watching, and Ariana captured it perfectly.

CHAPTER ONE

THE EARLY YEARS

Sometimes, parents spot very early on the direction their child's life will take. Little hints and signals begin to show themselves here and there; eventually they begin to form a trend that snowballs, and points to a possible future. But in the earliest years of Ariana Grande's life, her mother, Joan, was not wondering if her daughter would take a musical path. Instead, she feared her little girl was set for a darker direction.

As for Ariana, she knew just how her mother felt. 'There was a stage, when I was three or four, where my mom thought I might grow up to be a serial killer,' she joked in *Billboard* of her earliest years. Although the pop princess was exaggerating for comic effect, as is her wont in so many interviews, her description of her childhood interests as 'dark and deranged' has a hint of truth.

Looking back, she remembers how she enjoyed painting her face to make herself look like a skeleton. She would also often be seen wearing a Freddy Krueger mask, the serial killer from *A Nightmare on Elm Street* from the 1980s, who used his razor-bearing glove to kill people. Krueger's burned, disfigured face, his stripy jumper, brown fedora hat and trademark metal-clawed hand terrified audiences who saw the strictly adult-rated film. His murderous antics were not ones that many little girls were meant to see.

It was a gory and grown-up movie for Ariana to take to, but she has always had a taste for the scarier pictures. For instance, from her early years she loved *Jaws* and *Jurassic Park*. Directed by Steven Spielberg, *Jaws* was one of the biggest hit films of the 1970s, but not one that was intended for young eyes. A gripping movie, it features a huge man-eating shark that terrifies beach-goers in New England, USA. Its soundtrack has become synonymous with suspense and terror. Indeed, more squeamish adults struggled to stay the course of the movie because of the level of tension, and many who watched the film found themselves too scared to swim in the sea for years afterwards. Young Ariana, however, showed steel beyond her years in being able to stomach it.

Her other childhood favourite, *Jurassic Park*, was released in the year of her birth and is a less sinister film – yet still graphic in its own way. Again directed by Spielberg, this 1993 flick was set in a vast park inhabited by dinosaurs that had been cloned from ancient DNA. Although *Jurassic Park* is a more family-friendly film than *Jaws*, neither were made with younger children in mind. That Ariana watched and enjoyed them suggests she was a discerning viewer and knew what she liked, even in her early years, and that in some senses, at least, she was not on the most restrictive of parental leashes.

Her parents were indeed liberal when it came to Ariana's exposure to adult culture. Even family outings sometimes saw Ariana take in some grown-up art. 'When I was seven years old, my mom took me to see *Rocky Horror*,' she told *Time* magazine. 'That's just how my family is. We're just this Italian family that loves slightly raunchy humor.'

The family were well off and based in the upwardly mobile Les Jardins area of Boca Raton, a Floridian coastal town. Ariana remembers the house as 'a perfect home to grow up in'. She added that she would 'always have so many positive memories of it personally and professionally, from our annual Christmas Eve party and family reunions, to a great pool party we hosted when I graduated middle school'.

Although Ariana describes her family as simply 'Italian', her ancestors come from a wider and more varied background than some fans and, indeed, Ariana realized. According to an ancestry website, her father Edward's parents were Anthony Vincent Charles Butera (son of Charles A. Butera and Marie) and Florence P. Citrano. Charles is recorded to have been born in New Jersey to Italian parents Antonino Butera and Margherita Azzara, who were from Menfi, Provincia di Agrigento, Sicily. While some have assumed Ariana is Latino, and she herself has stated on Twitter, in response to a fan's question about her background, that 'I am Italian American, half Sicilian and half Abruzzese' – Sicily and Abruzzo both being regions in Italy –Ariana is not an Italian pure-bred.

In 2014 she revealed that her background is broader than she originally thought. 'just found out my grandparents are heavily greek and part north african … i thought i was Italian … who am i ? my whole life is a lie,' she quipped. In fact, it is not uncommon for those of Sicilian descent to sometimes have Greek or North African ancestry.

A number of Italy's sons and daughters have made small but memorable contributions to American music – some of the biggest names in music have Italian ancestry. The first wave of Italian pop idols were first- or second-generation American immigrants such as Frank Sinatra, Dean Martin, Tony Bennett and Mario Lanza. Adriano Celentano took a rockier edge. Although modern pop stars like Britney Spears, Selena Gomez and Gwen Stefani have some Italian blood – and the parents of Ariana's childhood musical hero,

Madonna, were Italian immigrants – the country is arguably still better known for its opera than its pop.

Ariana is the latest Italian American sensation, something her mother Joan, chief executive of a telephone and alarm system company named Hose-McCann Communications, could never have predicted for her daughter. Born on 11 June 1968, Joan Grande was the sort of mother young girls dream of having: by all accounts a hip, down-to-earth character who understood the ways and wants of the younger generation. MTV described her as 'one of the raddest moms out there' and 'one of the coolest celeb moms'.

Ariana's father, Edward Butera, is the founder and owner of a company called IBI Designs, Inc. Its website explains that Edward's studio is composed of 'a small group of graphic designers, web designers, professional photographers, and recently added – videographers', all of whom have a 'special passion' for their craft. He is clearly proud of his firm, and loves to express his artistic side, enjoying photography, graphic design and art outside of his working life, too. Ed is also a keen fisherman, often proudly sharing on social media photos and videos from his trips.

His dream of a career in design began in his school days and determined where he went for higher education. Born on 20 September 1958 and raised in Maplewood, New Jersey, he went on to study advertising and design at the New York Institute of

Technology. Moving between various design companies in New York and New Jersey, he met Joan at one such institution and the rest, as they say, is history.

They could not have known that this meeting would ultimately affect the lives of millions of people, many yet to be born, around the globe. The couple married, and Joan became pregnant with Ariana while she was still living in Brooklyn, New York; by the time she gave birth they had moved to Deerfield Beach in Florida, the sunshine state of America.

Ariana said she loved growing up in Florida. 'It was a great place to grow up. I grew up going to the beach all the time and having a lot of fun with my friends.' She experimented with sand art at Boca Raton's Sixth Annual Spring Fling at Mizner Park, an event that was described as a cross between 'a children's festival and an egg search' by the *Sun-Sentinel* newspaper.

Ariana's name was inspired by the character Princess Oriana from the 1980s animation movie *Felix the Cat*. Released in the US in 1991, the film sees a villainous scientist called Duke of Zill employ his robotic army to seize control of the Land of Oriana. The hero of the piece, Felix the Cat, leaps into action to save Princess Oriana and her land. The film was not universally popular, but with its musical score and happy ending, it won over some viewers, including, presumably, Joan and Edward. Her maternal grandfather had another name for her – 'Bellissima', which means 'most beautiful'. Some of her friends and fans refer to her simply as 'Ari'.

Ariana was not the only youngster in the household; Joan had a son, Frankie, from a previous marriage. That was to Doctor Victor Marchione, a pulmonologist (someone who focuses on the health of the respiratory system). Doctor Victor's work led to him taking a direct approach to the topic of smoking, especially when educating his son. Frankie remembers how when he was still a little boy, his father took him into the hospital and showed him a black lung. 'He wrung the lung out in front of me and I watched the black tar that killed its previous owner spill into a tray right in front of my face,' he told *Advocate* magazine.

Young Frankie immediately vowed that he would never touch a cigarette and he made it part of his 'life's mission' to deter others from smoking. Even at the age of five, Frankie unabashedly told a couple who were smoking in a restaurant that they were 'going to die'. This encounter came in the late 1980s, when awareness of the dangers of smoking was far less widespread than it is today – clearly Frankie was a very confident, self-aware child.

Ariana and Frankie (who is ten years older than his half-sister) both attended Pine Crest School in Broward County. A private prep school, it has campuses in Fort Lauderdale and Boca Raton. The latter, where Ariana and Frankie attended, is the William J. McMillan

Campus. They are the school's most famous graduates; *Frasier* actor Kelsey Grammer is the school's other well-known alumnus.

Like Ariana, Frankie also has a half-brother – James Marchione. A sporty young man, James is a fan of baseball and is the son of Doctor Victor.

An early photo of Ariana and Frankie shows him affectionately kissing her. Sharing the photo after she had found the full flush of fame, Ariana described her half-brother as 'a bundle of sparkles and bright, beautiful energy'. Another shows them dressed up and frolicking on Halloween. 'I adored and worshipped my brother, Frankie, as a little girl – everything he did was cool,' she says. 'My brother was always the one in the spotlight and I liked that,' she told *Billboard*. 'It was like he was the entertainment for me.'

Ariana, as the youngest in her family, was always set to be considered the baby – the one everyone looks out for. According to Linda Blair's book *Birth Order: What Your Position in the Family Really Tells You About Your Character*, this is because, as the youngest, no one has ever come along to take her role as the baby of the pack. According to Blair, last-borns often also have an 'outgoing, charming and cute nature', all of which applies to Ariana and aids her as an entertainer. These traits come about partly because, as the youngest, Ariana will have needed to find a new way to be as attractive and attention-grabbing as the rest of the family.

Furthermore, if the child is rewarded for their charm or neediness, they are unlikely to see any reason to change their behaviour, argues Blair. Creativity is a big part of the life of many last-borns such as Ariana, partly because their sometimes disorganized natures push them in that direction. They are also often rebellious and willing to try new things, as they are more inclined to test rules and boundaries.

On a sadder note, last-borns can be vulnerable to feelings of inferiority and low self-esteem because they were surrounded by people who were bigger, older and more advanced than them. This sometimes leads them to conclude early in life that they are less competent than others, when in reality they are merely younger and less experienced. They can also feel let down easily because they tend to be looked after closely later into their childhood. While Ariana certainly was well cared for, there is little evidence of any lack of self-belief.

As a Cancerian, Ariana has a typically offbeat sense of humour, shows a loyalty to her family, a reliability to friends and is very honest. Those born under this sign are also said to be tenacious and imaginative. On the less positive side, Cancerians can be grumpy, suspicious, manipulative and insecure.

As we have seen, Ariana had, by her own admission, a slightly devilish side as a child. This was not just because of her pop-culture interests. This may have been exaggerated by the fact that Ariana believes she is hypoglycaemic, so sometimes gets 'anxious' if she forgets to eat. Hypoglycaemia sets in when the level of glucose present in the blood falls below a set point. This makes people exhausted, dizzy, or just plain grumpy. Ariana told *Billboard*: 'When I was a little girl, I would turn into the Tasmanian devil.'

In fact, although Ariana has said that some of her interests as a child disturbed her mother, and Joan has herself backed up that assertion, elsewhere she has said that Joan approved of her darker side. 'She was like, "Yeah, my kid is rad!"' Ariana told the *Daily Telegraph*. Like mother, like daughter: Joan, too, was said to have had a dark side when she was a child and a pinch of this carried on into her adult life and motherhood. 'I've never seen her wear anything but black,' says Ariana of her mother. 'She says it's a part of who she is. A psychic she saw when she was younger told her that black was her colour. So she really decided to run with that one, I guess!'

However, Ed, Ariana's father, was not so sure about all this flirtation with darkness and horror. Ariana described her Dad's take on it all when, recalling herself as a 'messed-up little kid', she told *Billboard* about a night he came home late from work to find that Joan and Ariana had their faces made-up to look like skeletons. 'He was like, "Is this Halloween?" Nope, it's just another Wednesday in our house.'

There were very few dull moments in the Grande

household. And Ariana's fascination with horror made her stand out in her earliest years in the bright and sunny surroundings of Florida. Yet she adored the local scene, describing the neighbourhood she grew up in as a 'really fun little city'.

It was here also that the first bit of groundwork for her extraordinary pop career was laid. She remembers a recording studio 'next to my room, which helped launch my music career. I hope whoever purchases the home will have as many wonderful experiences as I did.' Joan, too, remembers the household fondly: 'This house was made for a family that loves to welcome others into their home,' she said. 'Some of the happiest moments of my life were in this house; my parents' eightieth birthday party, sleepover nights in the theater room watching movies with our kids, and using the observatory to witness a total eclipse.' Ariana continues to hold the area in enormous affection. 'The most relaxing thing to me is going to the beach at night,' she says. 'I mostly do [that] in Boca.'

The preoccupations and themes of Ariana's childhood make for a curious mix: as well as beach-life and adult-targeted entertainment, religion was a factor in Ariana's early life. Although she would later distance herself from the faith, she was raised a Roman Catholic, which helped to bring the family together for a while at least in this busy, bustling household.

Relations with her father Edward have been somewhat strained in recent times, as we shall see in future chapters, with Ariana referring to her manager as a step-dad, which some have read as a way of diminishing her real father's stature. Yet she does continue to say positive things about Edward. 'I am made up of half my dad, and a lot of my traits come from him,' Ariana told *Seventeen*. She also says she still loves her dad.

She loved her music, too. The soundtrack to Ariana's youth included the material of some huge musical stars. 'Growing up, I was listening to Whitney Houston all the time,' she said in 2013. '*The Bodyguard* soundtrack, a lot of Judy Garland and oldies, and divas.' Curiously, the two standout artists in the soundtrack of Ariana's childhood both faced tragic lives.

Judy Garland was a singer and actress whose career spanned four decades. Her influence continues to this day. However, her life had tragedy too. She signed her first movie contract at thirteen years of age. In 1939, she appeared in the film classic *The Wizard of Oz*, a part that would bring her huge international fame. Her rendition of the song 'Over the Rainbow', about a yearning for future happiness, became almost an emblem for her life. However, she was dropped by MGM Studios in the 1950s and then concentrated more on singing. She died in 1969 from an accidental drug overdose.

Whitney Houston, too, combined a life as one of the celebrated female singers of all time – with hits including 'I Will Always Love You' and 'Saving All My Love For You' – and enormous tragedy, culminating in an early death. She died in her guest room at the Beverly Hilton, in Beverly Hills, California in 2012.

Ariana also loved Madonna, as she told *Cosmopolitan* in 2017. 'I have the utmost respect for that woman,' she said. 'I love her with every ounce of my being, and not just because of her ability to outlast the blatant bullying and bullshit that she's had to put up with or because I'm obsessed with her entire discography. I'm so inspired by her bravery and her strength. I can look at her and not be scared to be strong.' Ariana would subsequently tread a similar path to Madonna in both her professional and spiritual life, as well as sharing a stage show with her.

But before any of that could happen, Ariana began to wonder how she could make it as a singer. She wanted to be famous. Showing her enterprising side, she decided, at the age of just four, to hit the phone and see what she could discover. 'I called 411, and asked to speak to Nick studios,' she said. 'They connected me and I told a receptionist I wanted to be on *All That* [an American live-action, sketch comedy/variety show on Nickelodeon]. She said I needed an agent.'

Music and Nickelodeon would ultimately catapult Ariana to fame. But her first public exposure came about through her love of sport. According to a 1998 report in the *Sun-Sentinel* newspaper, the 'real cutie' Ariana, then five, had gone to 'just about every home game' of the local ice hockey team, the Florida Panthers, since her second birthday. However, this virtual omnipresence at the matches would bring with it a physical price: in something of a bizarre coincidence, she was hit by the hockey puck on two occasions.

The first instance, in January 1998, saw her hit on the right wrist by an errant shot by the player Gord Murphy. The team felt so guilty about what happened that they gave Ariana various pieces of equipment as a gesture of goodwill. Then, in October of the same year, just as Joan was telling a *South Florida Insider* reporter about the January incident, incredibly, it happened again. This time, the offending puck had been fired by an unidentified member of the opposition, Tampa Bay. It hit Ariana in the left wrist. Joan and Edward immediately rushed her to the nearest first-aid station. There, an ice pack was applied to the small bruise on her left wrist. Edward, slightly shaken, asked: 'What are the odds of this happening?'

Although there were no pieces of sports equipment offered to Ariana on this occasion, she did enjoy one big treat at the game: during the first intermission, she became the first kid of the season to ride the Zamboni ice resurfacer. According to reports, she very much enjoyed the experience, 'waving at fans like a queen taking a horse and carriage ride'. Joan was delighted to see her daughter so happy, as she had paid $200 for the experience at an auction. Ariana had just had her first taste of fame. She liked it.

CHAPTER TWO

A FLAIR FOR THE THEATRE

From the outside, it is all too easy to imagine that a successful pop musician would spend her childhood years being trained hard to understand the intricacies of music, spending her every waking hour sweating over instruments, sheet music and vocal sessions, perhaps with a pushy parent or musical coach in the background.

But to listen to Ariana, it was a little more random than that for her. 'Music just kind of happened, I never really trained for anything,' she told *Complex* in 2013. She says that she played French horn for a few years, 'and that's where I learned a lot about sheet music and theory', but insists that she was never trained in singing or, to any significant extent, instrumental music.

Instead, her first steps in the performing arts were as

much about acting as singing. She joined a community theatre in Boca, which Joan was involved in as a board member. Ari got a leg up, and soon she would take the lead role in their production of the musical *Annie* and delight audiences. She had been very much influenced by her half-brother. 'Once Frankie got into acting in musical theatre and dancing, I was like, "OK, I guess that's the cool thing now, so let's investigate and watch old musicals,"' she told the *Daily Telegraph*. 'My friends and I were huge musical-theatre geeks and we would go back and forth to New York whenever we had free weekends.'

Her mother became a co-star, initially out of a sense of safety. Because she was still 'so young', remembered Ariana, Joan didn't want to leave her at the rehearsals alone, she says. 'But you weren't allowed to have your parents there unless they were in the show,' she continued. 'So my mom auditioned, which was the funniest thing that's ever happened in the history of the world!' To Ariana's further amusement, Joan successfully got the part – as Daddy Warbucks' maid. 'She had to wear a French maid's outfit and use a broom,' recalled Ariana. 'She was like, "I have no idea what I'm doing right now … but anything for my daughter."'

By all accounts Joan was a truly encouraging mother. As the author Julia Cameron explains in her seminal book about creativity, *The Artist's Way*, the encouragement children receive for their creative side shapes their happiness and success hugely. Joan is a dedicated mother, and her efforts were reflected in the way Ariana acted on and off the stage. She showed true star quality in a big production. When an eight-year-old girl can handle autograph hunters, backstage interviews and the performance itself with aplomb, you know she is going to take to stardom with ease. Ariana managed all of this in her role as the lead in the local production of *Annie*. Children's performances in plays often receive encouraging praise regardless of quality, but in the case of Ariana's tackling of Annie in 2001, she deserved every plaudit she received – and there were many.

The musical centres on the titular Annie, a feisty eleven-year-old orphan, who steals the hearts of the audience as they experience her rise from the Lower East Side of Manhattan. Determined to find her parents, she also rubs up against the evil head of the orphanage, Miss Hannigan. In the end, she finds a new family with the Depression-era billionaire Oliver Warbucks. With con artists and kidnap plots, the story has its dark turns, but this long-standing favourite of theatre and cinemagoers ends happily for Annie. With songs like 'It's the Hard-Knock Life', 'Tomorrow' and 'Maybe', it is an iconic and powerful story. As for Ariana, she had more than vindicated those who cast her in the role.

Her performances and backstage interactions were caught on video and are on the internet. Ariana – as

Annie – sings the song 'Tomorrow', where her fans now swell viewing figures far beyond what could have been imagined at the time. The performance took place at Little Palm Family Theater in Boca Raton, Florida, as part of a long-standing children's troupe that Ariana's mother and grandfather took over after it had begun to struggle financially. Dressed up with a natty outfit and complete with dirt rubbed on to her face and a curly red wig, Ariana looks the part in the video – and she sounds it, too.

She confidently looks out into the audience, even raising a cheeky eyebrow at a few points. Her interactions with other actors old and young, including one in a dog costume, are assured. She moves between the spoken and sung parts with ease. Even the big notes work well. It's safe to say that Ariana is a worthy lead, especially given her young age. No wonder the audience applause is so strong.

In a backstage interview on the video, Joan is seen talking about the experience. 'It's truly unbelievable,' she says, and praised the 'incredibly wonderful people' who also took part in the show. She said, 'as Ariana's mother, you can never imagine how it's been [to participate in the production]' and to spend time with her. 'There are no words to describe what this means to me as a parent.' Pride indeed.

However, Ariana didn't feel that her mother's enthusiasm spilled over into pushiness. 'I never had a stage mom,' she said later. The stage mother has become a cultural archetype – an unpleasantly pushy figure in the life of a child performer. They are often said to put unfair amounts of pressure on their child to reach the top, often because, it is believed, the stage mom is trying to live out her own dreams through the child. But Ariana says Joan was quite different. 'My mom is a businesswoman and she's awesome, and she was always like, "Whatever you want to do, I'll be here." She was very supportive throughout the whole thing. So thanks, mom.'

Indeed, in a separate interview, Ariana heaped so much praise on Joan that it became a touching, emotional tribute. 'Since I was a little girl, my mom would make me feel like I was a little star,' she told Neon Limelight. She explained that the grounding she received during these years would serve her well as her fame grows. 'It hasn't gone to my head or anything, but my mom has made me feel important since I was just a bumblebee in Billy Goats Gruff in my school production. So, it's like, you know, my mom has taken amazing care of me and she's just taught me so many amazing things that I feel like a lot of teenagers my age haven't been fortunate enough to learn yet.'

Edward also expressed pride on the video. He says that 'it's never quiet in our household' but it's 'a nice noise to hear your daughter sing and act all the time'. His commitment to his daughter's singing is clear as he tells of how he has 'never missed a show yet', and that he 'probably never will'. He says her participation 'keeps us singing around the house'. Then Joan asks Ariana if it's a great show, to which her daughter confidently replies: 'Uh huh.' However, for Ariana, the experience flew by so much faster than she had expected. 'It's so fun but it went by so fast and I'm so sad that it's over,' she says.

Later in the video Ariana is signing autographs for fans – something she would become very familiar with later in life. One fan offers the leading girl a bunch of flowers. She takes her newfound moment of fame with aplomb. It had been a wonderful and successful evening, though Ariana had expressed embarrassment when confronted by such videos. Much later, during an appearance on *The Tonight Show*, she said of her voice's development since then: 'I'm a little better!'

When asked by the *Daily Telegraph* whether the experience had proved a refuge for her, Ariana responded: 'Oh absolutely! Like, "Take me away from home." I remember saying, "Mommy, I never want this to end." I loved playing a character as it was sort of just taking a vacation from myself.'

There was trouble brewing at home, however – meaning there was plenty for Ariana to take shelter from. At the age of eight, Ariana's happy childhood faced its first big test. 'That was very hard as a young girl when my parents got divorced,' she told the *Daily Telegraph* in 2014. 'Being in the middle of it was so stressful.

And of course being made up of both of them – I was like, "Hey, if they both dislike each other's attributes so much, what am I to like about me? I'm made from these two people and I'm caught in the middle of all this fighting." It was traumatic. Between the ages of eight and eleven, that was the roughest for me.'

Experts recognize this sort of impact. Writing for *Psychology Today*, Carl E. Pickhardt explained: 'For the young child, divorce shakes trust in dependency on parents who now behave in an extremely undependable way. They surgically divide the family unit into two different households between which the child must learn to transit back and forth, for a while creating unfamiliarity, instability, and insecurity, never being able to be with one parent without having to be apart from the other.'

For Ariana, the disruption between her parents only made her closer to her grandparents. This would influence her musical tastes, which, like her cinematic ones, show a preference for older works. 'I have an obsession with all things vintage and classic and old-school, everything from Marlene Dietrich to Frankie Valli and The Four Seasons to Connie Francis,' she said. 'My grandpa was always telling me I should sing songs from the Great American Songbook.'

Ariana continued to enjoy the break from reality that theatre gave her, and there would be further musicals that would allow her to take a vacation from herself.

Next up came the lead role in the play that made her hero Judy Garland famous: *The Wizard of Oz*. This fulfilled an ambition Ariana had had for several years. 'It's exciting. I've always wanted to play Dorothy,' she told the *Sun-Sentinel* in 2003, giving a newspaper interview at the tender age of nine. '*The Wizard of Oz* has been my favorite movie since I was four.' Judy Garland was sixteen when she won the role of Dorothy in the MGM musical in 1938 and it was to mark the beginning of a long career. Time would tell if it proved the same for Ariana.

Joan, too, featured in that *Sun-Sentinel* article. The co-author of the script adaptation for the play, she had the role of one of the wicked witches. 'Last year, when Ariana played Annie, they suggested I participate since it was her first play. I did and it was the most rewarding time I've spent with her,' she said. 'My son Frankie is the dance captain, so it's truly a family affair.'

It was pertinent that *Oz* includes the song 'Over the Rainbow', the emotional musical centrepiece of the play. It is clear to see that in theatre Ariana had found that magical place where her troubles evaporated. Little could she know that she would one day sing the classic at a highly charged concert in the north of England.

The song, which was first recorded in 1938, is one of the most enduring of the twentieth century. After *The Wizard of Oz* became a hit, the track won the

Academy Award for Best Original Song and became Judy Garland's signature piece.

Ariana performed in another well-known play, *Beauty and the Beast*. She later described that production, along with *Annie* and *The Wizard of Oz*, as 'those cute plays' that she took part in before she was 'taking it seriously'. Perhaps she was underselling the level of her childhood professionalism, as she later told *Billboard* magazine, 'I just wanted to do every single show ... However many there were in a year, I was in every one, whether I was a chorus girl or the lead or doing the lighting.' She was working hard in these musicals and enjoying herself as she did. Thanks in large part to Joan's carefully balanced support, Ariana was able to gain a successful and healthy momentum as she chased her dreams. Further breaks were coming her way, including from a fortuitous neighbour.

The family lived next door to a man called Dennis Lambert, who Ariana got to know when she was eleven or twelve, as he was the father of her friend Misha. The two girls met when Misha became involved in the Little Palm Theater. Lambert has since told a local newspaper, the *Palm Beach Post*, that he spotted Ariana's potential from the start. 'I felt, and everyone in my family felt, she was going to be a star,' he said. 'She was always an amazing little talent in person. She knows how to deliver.'

Lambert knows his stuff: he has produced and co-written big hits, including Glen Campbell's 'Rhinestone Cowboy' and the Four Tops' 'Ain't No Woman'. He also played parts in the tracks 'It Only Takes a Minute', 'We Built This City', 'Night Shift' and 'One Tin Soldier'. A documentary entitled *Of All the Things* was even once made about him: he was a hugely encouraging neighbour for the Grandes to have.

He remembered Ariana as an 'amazing singer' as a young child. 'She could sing like Mariah Carey even back then, with that wonderful head voice, and the ability to mimic or copy all the singers she admired.' He added that Ariana could 'copy all their licks, before she got her own sense of what to do'. Praise indeed.

Little Palm Theater was a very important place for the Grande family, several members having deep roots there. (Her grandfather, Frank, won a 'Men with Caring Hearts' award for his volunteer work at the Little Palm Theater, where he was president of the board of directors.) Yet eventually, the theatre closed – but this was not to stop Ariana and her mother in their tracks. Joan formed a small children's troupe of around eight youngsters called Kids Who Care. Its number included her daughter and Ariana's friend Misha, as well as Aaron Simon Gross, who would later co-star with Ariana on Broadway.

The troupe sang at charity events, raising funds for a host of good causes. Misha's father Dennis recalls that Kids Who Care would perform at 'black tie affairs in an effort to raise money, get exposure and be a part of a philanthropic sense of giving something back'. He sometimes played a part himself, allowing his daughter and her friends to perform songs of his. He also arranged a special holiday performance. Ariana's charitable spark was being fanned into a blaze early in life. The youth singing group raised over $500,000 for charities in 2007 alone. Charity has always been an important part of Ariana's career and life, and it was in her childhood in Florida that Joan drummed this admirable trait into her.

Dennis was not the only musical talent to offer her encouragement – a superstar had added her own words of encouragement when Ariana was a few years younger. The legendary Latino singer Gloria Estefan also weighed in. Starting off in bands, Estefan was originally lead singer in a group called Miami Latin Boys. She then became a solo star, shifting more than 100 million records, including the hit singles 'Get On Your Feet', 'Rhythm Is Gonna Get You', 'Anything For You', '1-2-3' and 'Don't Wanna Lose You'. Quite a talent to stumble upon by accident – yet that is exactly what happened.

The two crossed paths when Ariana's family were holidaying on a cruise ship. Ariana enjoyed singing karaoke during the trip, and on one day she was singing the Celine Dion hit 'My Heart Will Go On'. 'It was a terrible song choice,' Ariana admitted later, on Alan

Carr's show *Chatty Man*. '[A] really dark choice, but I was only six or seven so I didn't know what I was doing.' After she had finished the song, Ariana was in for quite a surprise. Someone approached her and said: 'Gloria Estefan would like to speak to you'.

Ariana was, quite naturally, stunned. 'I was like, "are you serious?" and my brother was like, "Are you f**king serious?" And we went together to go say hi to her.' Ariana was so excited. Estefan told her: 'I just want to let you know that you are so talented and do not ever give up'. The singer added that Ariana had so much more than she did at that age, and that she must keep going because Ariana was 'meant to do this'. What an experience. 'It was crazy,' recalled Ariana. She added that Estefan inspired her, and that the encounter gave her further encouragement to pursue her musical ambitions.

Estefan herself also remembers the exchange and how impressed she had been with Ariana. She told the *New York Daily News*, 'I literally went up to her and told her and her mom, "I don't know if you plan on doing this, but this is what you need to be doing because you are an amazing singer."' Ariana sums up the incident now by saying that Estefan 'kind of' discovered her – quite a feather in the cap for both women!

Before she even hit her teens, Ariana had already performed with several South Florida orchestral ensembles, as her official book *Ariana: The Book* explains.

•

She also filmed a pilot television show. Alongside other young acting talent – twelve-year-olds Preston Bryan and Dylan Lerner – and under the watchful eye of South Florida philanthropist Flossy Keesely, she went to the studios of Information Television Network in Boca Raton. The broadcasting company produced the *E-Venture Kids* pilot show, which was due to air on PBS. That phone call she made as a hopeful four-year-old was clearly paying off.

Ariana's performing talents were many: she also showed her capacity for humour and impersonation. 'I did stand-up for my grandparents every day when I was eight,' she said. The seeds for her well-known *Saturday Night Live* comedy pieces were being sown before she had even reached double figures.

She was making strides on several fronts, and she still had the benefit of an industry-savvy neighbour. Although he had lots of industry know-how, Lambert decided not to bombard Ariana and her mother with advice, as he felt Joan seemed to be navigating her daughter's career well. Some such luminaries as him would feel compelled to offer tips – perhaps out of kindness – but Lambert felt it best not to.

He did offer one nugget, though: think beyond their local neighbourhood. 'The only advice I ever remember giving her mother was to not fall for the idea that someone in your backyard was going to be the right fit, because they're not probably gonna be the right person, and that includes me,' he told PalmBeachPost.com. 'Boca has a lot of people with a pedigree, most of whom were older, and I didn't think any of those people were the right [ones] for her, as talented as they may be.'

Ariana's national television vocal debut had been in 2001, when she sang the 'Star-Spangled Banner' at a Florida Panthers hockey game. This was a phenomenal gig for a youngster to get. To entrust such a tender-aged girl to tackle the song in front of a live and television audience was a bold move – but Ariana was not about to let them down. Sharing a glimpse into her talent and self-assurance as a vocalist, she did herself and her family proud.

For television viewers, the match-day commentator introduced the starlet as he invited the audience to 'join Ariana Grande-Butera as she honours America, with the singing of our national anthem'. And so she appeared: standing under a spotlight and dressed in black, she looked dramatic. She held the microphone, on its stand, with both hands, singing the song slowly as flag-brandishing servicemen looked on. What an assured performance it was.

When she reached the famous 'land of the free' hook at the song's climax, the audience applauded and roared its approval. Although she had looked nervous at points during the song, gulping here and there, with the final note sung she backs away confidently from the microphone, with a huge smile on her face. 'Nicely done,' says the television commentator, 'Ariana Grande-Butera with the national anthem'.

Nicely done indeed. It has been an accomplished performance from Ariana, and one can only imagine the pride of her family and the girl herself after she performed it so well. 'Hahahh, enjoy!' wrote Ariana when, in 2011, she shared the video with her fans on her Facebook page. Ariana was certainly enjoying her music and the other elements of her performance. A star was in the making.

CHAPTER THREE

HER FIRST BIG BREAK

When one examines the childhoods of those who become a phenomenon in their chosen field, we can often find key moments in which they succeed and those whose focus and drive is ultimately only slightly weaker fade away; the gap between success and failure can frequently be slim. Lots of kids dream of becoming a singer, but for many the ambition never moves beyond daydreaming, or holding a hairbrush in place of a pretend microphone in their bedroom. Often, the ones who hit the heights will show some signs of that stronger determination early on.

Ariana did that, messing about with a digital musical plaything from her early years. 'I've always loved music,' she told *Complex*. 'I was just always writing growing up and making cute songs with GarageBand ... music was always such a massive part of my life; it's my passion.' GarageBand is a piece of software that lets users turn their phone, tablet or computer into a recording studio, complete with a vast collection of musical instruments. She also used a Boss RC-50 Loop Station. Made famous most recently by British singer-songwriter Ed Sheeran, loop pedals allow the user to record a few bars of music, which then repeat – or loop – while the user plays other parts over the top. The loop pedal sometimes confuses audiences when used live: Sheeran has found himself repeatedly having to explain that, no, he is not miming to a backing track, but is in fact building that track himself, live on stage.

It's easy to pinpoint the inspiration for all of this: both of the tools Ariana used had been employed by one of her earliest heroes, Imogen Heap. An award-winning songwriter and performer, Heap has released four solo albums that enjoyed commercial success in the UK and the US. She is also quite the innovator: Imogen was the first female artist to win a Grammy for Best Engineered Album. She also designed and made musical gloves that allow the wearer to sculpt and manipulate sound on and off stage with gestures.

Ariana loved her. She started writing songs at the age of ten, as she explained later to Neon Limelight. 'The first song I ever wrote was really silly, and I still actually have it on my computer, which is really funny,' she said. 'It was about rain. Like, just about rain. No deeper meaning, no subtext, just rain. I was really young when I wrote it, too. I don't know why I never thought about writing songs before age ten, but I guess I just always liked singing other artists' songs until ten, then I was like, oh well, and tried and it was really funny.'

Amid all this early musical experimentation and technology, Ariana's confidence built – and then some. So much so that when she travelled to Los Angeles as a teenager to meet some musical managers, she had her path all worked out in her head. The trouble was that when she expressed it out loud, she got something of a reality check from the industry chiefs. Now, she laughs when she looks back on it. 'When I was fourteen, I wanted to make a straight-up, like, India Arie record,' remembers Ariana, laughing. 'Something really soulful.' Her attraction to soul came, she believes, from a mystical realm. 'I honestly think it could be a past-life thing,' she said. 'You know those things where you love something but you don't know why, or you're scared of something but you don't know why? I feel like all of those things are from another life.'

She told *Billboard*, 'I remember when I first came to LA to meet with my managers, I was like, "I want to make an R&B album". They were like: "Um, that's a hell of a goal! Who is going to buy a fourteen-year-old's R&B album?!"' They were not buying her ideas at this stage, so there was no fourteen-year-old Ariana album.

Instead, she returned to the stage, when she was cast in

the role of Charlotte the cheerleader in the musical play *13*. The storyline sees young Evan Goldman struggling with a pile-up of issues after his family moved from New York City to small-town Indiana. Evan has to deal with his parents' divorce and prepare for his impending bar mitzvah, the Jewish rite of passage for teenage boys. Meanwhile, he also has to cope with settling in at a new school, with all the social and emotional pressures that process can bring.

When it opened in New York in 2008, the play made history immediately because it was the first Broadway musical ever with a cast and band entirely comprised of teenagers. But it had endured quite a journey to get to New York's famous, winding theatrical thoroughfare. 'I was a part of the project for a really long time,' Ariana said, looking back. Originally, the play had enjoyed a short run at the Mark Taper Forum theatre in Los Angeles in early 2007. Ariana was not part of that staging, 'but then they brought it to New York and we did a reading and it started there'.

'I was involved with *13* for almost a year. It was so different then, I really enjoyed being a part of the process all the way through because I got to be a part of the changes,' she said. 'It was crazy how much it changed. In the reading we were all playing six different parts. I had to be a rapper, I had to be an old grandma, it was just so fun.'

It actually arrived on Broadway via a month-long

stop-off at the Norma Terris Theatre in Chester, Connecticut, in May 2008, opening on Broadway at the Bernard B. Jacobs Theatre on 16 September with previews before the official opening on 5 October. After 105 performances and 22 previews, it closed on 4 January 2009.

Broadway is the oldest north–south main thoroughfare in New York City – but that is its least impressive claim to fame. It is the home of the world's most famous theatre district. Oscar Hammerstein kicked things off when he built his Victoria Theater on West 42nd Street, and it has since turned into the heart of New York's entertainment industry. For more than 100 years Broadway has been launching young talent on to the world, as well as, of course, featuring more established stars.

Ariana, who said she had 'grown up with my mom taking me to Broadway shows', became the latest in that tradition. Key to her enjoyment of the experience was the presence of her best friend, Aaron. 'I was very fortunate to do *13* with him,' she said. 'We [have been] friends since we were, like, six years old and it's just so crazy ironic that we were both cast; these two kids from Boca, in a Broadway musical together.'

As *13*'s Manhattan run continued, Ariana came to the attention of several journalists as they arrived to review the performance. The *New York Times* offered a thorough write-up. Ben Brantley speculated that he couldn't 'imagine that anyone who isn't in early adolescence would be crazy about *13*'. However, he added that the production has a 'buoyant score' and 'certainly has on tap that natural radioactive energy that makes young teenagers so appealing and so scary'.

A fourteen-year-old performing arts student who accompanied Brantley to the play was more complimentary, citing 'polished singing' and musicians with 'undeniable flair'. He also praised its 'clever lyrics and genuinely funny jokes'. Although Ariana was not mentioned directly in the review, her name was listed at the foot of the article, where the cast and crew were each namechecked.

Ariana herself namechecked Brantley during an interview with the Florida *Sun Sentinel*. 'During the rehearsal process it was hard to believe we were on Broadway because it's an all teen cast, and it felt like we were just partying all the time. But then when we opened, and it was like, "Hey, Ben Brantley."'

She had been thrown in at the deep end but she found the experience amazing: exhilarating and exciting all at once. 'You would think that it would be totally exhausting and, at some points, it was,' she said. 'But there was never a night where it [was] like, "I want to do another show." It was amazing.'

But, as she told Neon Limelight, 'there are plenty of hardships' that come along with performing on stage. She describes how, from middle school, she suddenly 'got thrown into the performance life'. She continued: 'I went right from middle school, like regular, everyday school, to Broadway. And that was a really crazy transition to make because it was so much hard work. I was like yay, no more school! Then I was like, oh my God, I have to kill myself every day dancing for more than twelve hours and sit on my couch every day with Icy Hot and Tiger Balm and the whole house smelling like menthol and just waiting for my muscle pain to go away.'

In a video of Ariana singing at a promotional ticket-sales event in Pittsburgh, the MC described *13* as 'a fantastic new musical' and the 'only teenage cast to ever hit Broadway'. Ariana won a National Youth Theatre Association Award for *13*, and in 2009 she received a knock-on benefit from her Broadway stint when she was invited to join other theatre stars for a web series called *The Battery's Down*. Her appearance was a brief cameo, which included her riffing at a bar mitzvah during the song 'All About Me' alongside her *13* and *Victorious* co-star Elizabeth Gillies.

Another co-star in *13* was to have a different kind of impact on Ariana's life. Graham Phillips, who played Evan in *13*, sang the song 'O Holy Night' with Ariana, and they also co-wrote and performed a song called 'Stick Around'. Soon, rumours would circulate that they had become an item. In 2010, the year after *13*'s Broadway run, they attended the Emmy Awards together. They were also spied together on the red carpet at the 2010 Broadway in South Africa Concert and then went to Laguna Beach together. She has hinted that Graham gave her her 'adorkable' first kiss when she was fourteen. He also showed up at Ariana's eighteenth birthday party at Paramount Studios in Los Angeles, and the couple were said to have dated for up to three years.

Later, on the seventh anniversary of the Broadway opening, in fact, she reminisced on Twitter about her time in *13*, explaining that she was 'so thankful for the friendships, the experience' and 'the music'. Thanking the musical mastermind behind the play, Jason Robert Brown, she said, 'I could sing your music all day, every day, forever.' Her co-star and friend Elizabeth Gillies also looked back. She tweeted that it was a 'magical experience that will always hold a special place in my heart'. She said she was 'So thankful for all the memories [and] friendships'. If it wasn't for *13*, she continued, she 'would never have met my lil' dingus' Ariana.

There were other theatrical openings for Ariana, who also appeared in Desmond Child's musical *Cuba Libre*. In an interview she gave during the work, she described it as 'so incredible', adding that working with Child was 'amazing – love you Desmond!!' She created the original role of Miriam. Looking ahead, she told *Backstage*, she had one big theatrical ambition. 'Well, I was in a Broadway show before, and I have to say that nothing would replace that feeling. It's one of the most amazing things in the entire world. But as far as dream roles – I know this is so expected of me, but I would love to play Elphaba in *Wicked* on Broadway. I have a lot of dream roles, but that's like my main one because of the vocal track. I love belting high things!' Although she has not, at the time of writing at least, fulfilled this ambition, on her second album she did inject a bit of *Wicked*.

There was one audition that didn't go so well for her, as she told *Backstage*. 'I had this one audition for a Broadway show. They did the dancing first, and I was all ready to dance and I was so excited. And I was really thrilled because I had done all the choreography correctly and I was like, "Thank, God. I'm so, so, so excited." … And they were cutting people straight from the audition and they said, "You have to go because you weren't silly enough." And I was like, "What?" And they were like, "You were supposed to make goofy faces." And I was like, "Excuse me?" And then that was it.'

By now, she had left school – and just at the right moment, as far as Ariana was concerned. 'I think that I left at a good time because I feel like that's when the mean girls all pop up,' she explained. 'I'm still enrolled at my school now in Florida, North Broward Preparatory School. They provide my material and then tutors teach it to me. I love them there for everything they're doing for me.' It was good timing for Ariana to leave behind conventional schooling – because a big opportunity was coming her way. She was about to move from the stage to the small screen.

For many stars of recent decades, Disney has been the television launch pad for their pop careers. Britney Spears, Christina Aguilera and Justin Timberlake are just a few of the idols who took that route, becoming stars of the 1990s pop scene and beyond. More recent Disney graduates include Miley Cyrus and Selena Gomez. Disney has produced some of Ariana's favourite singers and closest industry pals. Then there has been the reality television route. In the US, the chief production line in this sector has been the TV series *American Idol*, which has produced such industry figures as Kelly Clarkson, Ruben Studdard, Carrie Underwood, Taylor Hicks and Trent Harmon.

However, for Ariana, Nickelodeon was the springboard. A cable and satellite television network launched in the 1970s, Nickelodeon is aimed squarely at children and teenagers. After some testing times during its earlier decades, it is now something of a broadcasting powerhouse. By the time Ariana came to their notice, Nickelodeon was mammoth.

It was a sudden arrival into television. 'It all happened so quickly,' Grande told the *Sun-Sentinel*. 'It's like, one day I'm at school and then the bell rings and I had to go do an audition for *13* ... I've been so lucky. I'm so appreciative. I have an agent, and they put me up to it,' she explained. 'You know, you go into auditions and say, "Hopefully they like me". The original audition was [where] everybody had the same character, boy or girl, and you had to read the lines and act a little crazy.

'The audition process was really fun! I started the process in NY while I was doing *13* the Broadway musical and then my callback was in LA! Afterwards, I had a few screen tests and then I got the call from [producer] Dan Schneider himself telling me that I was going to play Cat! I almost died.' The audition for the series *Victorious* had proved to be just that. Ariana's part, Cat Valentine, was a classmate and friend of the series' protagonist Tori Vega (Victoria Justice).

Alongside her were several of her *13* cast mates, including Elizabeth Gillies, who later recalled the experience during an interview with *Seventeen*. 'We booked *Victorious* together, which was totally surreal,' said Gillies. 'This was the fourth consecutive job we had booked together. Ariana was the only person in the cast I knew beforehand, but it only took about a day for us all to really hit it off. I knew after the first day on set that our cast was going to be like a family and luckily I was right. We all get along really great.'

A situation-comedy set in a performing arts high school, *Victorious* was created and produced by Dan Schneider. 'If there is anything I've learned about kids today – and I'm not saying this is good or bad – it's that they all want to be stars,' said Schneider of his thinking behind the concept. He accepted that it would be positive if more youngsters 'wanted to be teachers and social workers' instead of celebrities, but continued: 'At least in *Victorious*, you see a world where they're all working on the talent part.'

Over the years, as the man behind a string of hits including *iCarly*, *Zoey 101*, *Drake & Josh*, *The Amanda Show* and *All That*, Schneider has established himself as a television hit maker. He has made a series of young actors and actresses famous, led by Miranda Cosgrove, who was the sixteen-year-old star of *iCarly*. Schneider is a serious player in the industry and expectations were high for the success of this new venture, meaning it offered Ariana a great platform to the world.

But this was not just another project for Schneider. Instead it was, as the *New York Times* put it, 'arguably the most ambitious project that Mr Schneider has undertaken'. Indeed, as Marjorie Cohn, then executive vice president for original programming and development at Nickelodeon, explained, the aim was to create a show on their network which could rival Disney's Miley Cyrus-starring *Hannah Montana* or Fox Broadcasting's *Glee*. Cohn said: What we really do best is to follow where kids are. Kids are into music, maybe more than ever, and we asked Dan to create a music-based show.'

As part of the step-up in expectation came a step-up in the age of the cast. The high school students in *Victorious* were more mature in years and in outlook than those in previous Schneider efforts. 'I think it's going to be cool for the audience to see a slightly older group of kids,' said Schneider of Ariana and her fellow cast members. 'But it's still a show that you can put the kids in front of and walk away and not worry about what they are going to see.'

Series one began filming on 5 October 2009. By the close of filming in April the following year, the earliest episodes had been shown. The network had considered the age range of the cast when arranging the set. Paula Kaplan, Nickelodeon's executive vice president for talent, told the *New York Times*: 'In our adult world, nobody accommodates us for down time. But in a child's life on a set, we do take that seriously. At our studios on Sunset Boulevard, where we shoot *iCarly* and *Victorious*, the green rooms are filled with games and Rock Band. We create an environment where they can have fun with their colleagues and take it easy.'

On its debut in March 2010, *Victorious* was watched by 5.7 million viewers. *Billboard* noted Cat's 'Tai-like frizzy red hair', and her 'idiosyncratic-to-be-generous fashion sense', as well as 'the tendency to break into hysterics at a moment's notice'. Writer Andrew Unterberger continued: 'It's virtually unrecognizable as the composed, stately, brunette Grande we've come to know from her performances and music videos.' *Variety* magazine's critic Brian Lowry wrote, '*Victorious* has been cobbled together with the wooden-headed market in mind.'

David Hinckley of the *New York Daily News* felt *Victorious* was too similar to *iCarly*, as 'likable fresh-faced students' navigate 'easily recognizable teen dramas'. He added: 'In general, it will be good if *Victorious* develops a little more distinctive personality over the next twenty episodes.' If that seems harsh, then it is as nothing compared to what Mark A. Perigard of the *Boston Herald* wrote. Headlining his review, '*Victorious* is a big loser', he wrote: 'The bulk of the cast mugs for the cameras, probably to compensate for a script that could have been commissioned from fifth-graders.' At least the *New York Post*, while calling *Victorious* 'corny', said it was a surefire hit.

In April of the following year came season two. In subsequent series, said *Billboard*'s Unterberger, Grande's character was less 'grating'. He wrote that she was 'still a little manic, but mostly just very impressionable and easily swayed – often confused and more than a little dim-witted, but generally sweet and well-meaning'. He also noted that Ariana 'rarely changes facial expressions or vocal tones throughout the entire show; whether Cat's ecstatic or furious, chilled-out or freaked out, she keeps the same innocent, moony-eyed look with the same soft, lilting monotone'. However, overall he felt that she 'slays' some scenes.

As *Billboard* continued of her acting effort overall: 'It seems like maybe Ariana doesn't have a ton of range as an actress yet, though she unquestionably has a good deal of charisma, and a generally sympathetic quality … Hopefully if and when she does get back to acting, she can play an adult sort of character – hopefully outside the Nick umbrella – so we can see what she's actually like as an actress.'

Ariana later compared stage acting with performing for the television cameras. Speaking to alloy.com, she said: 'Broadway is amazing because you're performing for such an intimate group of people. You're living in the moment and whatever happens happens, and you go on. You can't say cut and redo it, you have to be on the whole time. It's for a small group of people and you're feeding off their energy.' She added: 'When you're filming it's also really awesome because an audience of like a million people are going to see it. And you have to stay there the whole day and you get up really early and go into hair and makeup at the crack of dawn. It's really fun, both ways.'

Ariana described her character, Cat Valentine, during an interview with Modoration.Com: 'She's fun-loving, free-spirited, flighty and highly emotional! She loves singing and cute boys. She lives in her own world which she's created in her head and is always distracted by it. I love her!!' Sounded like someone close to home – as Ariana's interviewer suggested. 'I'm similar to Cat in a lot of ways actually! We're both fun-loving, free-spirited, silly and musical. I can also definitely relate to Cat's emotions, being a sixteen-year-old girl ... my mood swings certainly aren't as drastic as Cat's but I can totally understand where she's coming from.'

She said that the decision to dye her hair bright red came from Dan Schneider. 'It was totally genius and I can't see my character any other way. It's like deciding to become vegan. We did a flashback episode, and even young she had it. She made this decision early and it became part of her. And I have to thank Dan because it helps me play her. When I dyed my hair it gave me a new energy that I could bring into the character. It definitely helps.'

However, the experience did come with issues for Ariana, too, as she reflected later. 'I was adjusting to these new things – red carpets, and people wanting pictures with me, and people taking pictures of me when I didn't know they were being taken,' she told the *Daily Telegraph* in 2014. 'There was a lot of weird superficial nonsense that sprouted from it that I definitely wasn't used to. It was very weird. I just really liked performing.'

At the time, she also shared with the *Sun-Sentinel* how she was finding public recognition. Although she insisted she was enjoying everything about being famous, she added that: 'The overwhelming part is the recognition. I didn't expect anyone to recognize me in public. It just started happening and it's really cool.'

It had indeed started happening – and she described one such incident. 'Just today I was out to lunch with my mom and this woman was like, "I love your hair", and then she was like, "Oh my God! You're Cat!" She was at a table with her daughter and all her sixteen-year-old friends, and they all started screaming. And then they came over and gave me a cupcake. It was sweet.' However later she did admit to having issues with Cat, the character she had previously gushed over. 'For a long time I was attached to a character that was nothing like myself. It was a little frustrating.'

There were further ripples in her life when rumours emerged that she and actress Victoria Justice, who played Tori, had fallen out with one another while filming the show. A video of some of her *Victorious* co-stars surfaced, featuring Elizabeth Gillies and Daniella Monet commenting on how Grande 'sings everything'. Victoria Justice then snaps, 'I think we all sing'. This was interpreted as a swipe at Ariana. More upset came after Ariana briefly dated Jordan Viscomi, a *Victorious* backup dancer. After a few months together, the pair broke up and Arina admitted that it was a 'horrible, horrendous breakup'.

After *Victorious* came *Sam & Cat*, a crossover spin-off/sequel to both *Victorious* and its popular predecessor *iCarly*. Starring Jennette McCurdy as Sam Puckett and Ariana Grande as Cat Valentine, it saw the two characters meet by chance during a bizarre adventure and become room-mates, then start a babysitting business to earn extra money.

It aired on Nickleodeon from June 2013 to July 2014. When it was cancelled, the media offered up a series of different theories for the decision. One theory was that there was a dispute over salary between McCurdy and Nickelodeon, another cited a possible feud between McCurdy and Grande. Elsewhere it was claimed that a leak of revealing photographs of McCurdy was behind the decision. Other commentators speculated that Ariana's soaring musical career was what did for *Sam & Cat*, or that it was simply that she and McCurdy both wanted to move on to other projects.

Certainly, McCurdy's photo scandal did not help. It was a truly embarrassing moment for her, as she explained after she pulled out of the Kids' Choice Awards party. 'I wish I could explain everything as thoroughly as I would like to, but unfortunately a simpler explanation is all I can write,' she said in a statement. 'I was put in an uncomfortable, compromising, unfair situation (many of you have guessed what it is) and I had to look out for me.' Turning to Ariana's fan base, as well as her own, she added: 'I want to thank those of you who have reached out with kind words of support, McCurdians and Arianators alike. No matter who or what you support, I believe in supporting fairness first. If you have done that, thank you.'

Then there were there rumours that there was a civil war raging over salary – a suggestion that Ariana took to Twitter to deny. 'I hate addressing rumors and I hate gossip but this is really bothering me,' she began, on a 'Twitlonger' post. After explaining that the two leads had agreed from the start to be on equal pay, she said: 'The rumors circulating about our contracts and our salary not being equal are absolutely ridiculous and false. I don't know who's putting these idiotic quotes out there but I thought I'd straighten it out and try to end this nonsense.'

She continued: 'As far as the show goes, I don't know what's happening because I'm not directly involved with the problem but I just wanted to address this one rumor in particular because I am NOT making more money than my costar, nor do I think I should be.' For her, this rumour had stung because she is 'about equality and fairness'.

An eloquent rebuttal but not one that was enough to stem the chattering that the two actresses had fallen out. As many female celebrities find, it was being assumed that they had rowed and wrecked everything – an insidiously misogynistic view of life. Eventually, McCurdy came out strong in an interview with *E! News*, stating that those who looked for problems between her and Ariana were barking up the wrong tree. 'I just feel that Ariana and I were and are extremely close and extremely like-minded in a lot of different ways, and then sort of as the show dissolved everybody wanted to find some sort of hidden meaning in our relationship and some like drama, and I think we butted heads at times but in a very sisterly way. Like she knows me so well and I know her so well that I think it was unfortunate that things got misconstrued.'

The HelloGiggles website concluded that Ariana's character was, in fact, 'dangerous' to viewers. 'Cat is a walking talking barbie doll,' wrote Amy Foster. 'There is a long tradition of the lovable dimwits on TV and film: Gilligan, Shaggy, Forrest Gump, the Nutty Professor, Prince Charming's Dad in *Cinderella*, Homer Simpson, Phoebe from *Friends*, the guys from *Dumb and Dumber*, Adam Sandler in any movie he's ever done … The dangerous aspect of Cat is that there is a sexiness which underlines everything – that somehow intelligence is not needed as long as you look and dress a certain way.' Some would argue that Foster was taking the programme more seriously than intended, and perhaps overthinking it to a degree.

The higher-circulation *Los Angeles Times* was more glowing. 'For a particular audience, this will be epic,' wrote Robert Lloyd. Cat, he continued, 'is all pink and red' and 'has the attractive quality of being chronologically older and mentally younger than the target audience'. Amusingly, he also wrote: 'There is something at once endearing and annoying about the series, in which sense it is very like the demographic it has been designed to entertain and serve.'

Newsday said it was 'lively' and 'fun', forecasting:

'Kids will love it.' *Billboard*'s main criticism at least worked in Ariana's favour. 'It was one thing to see Cat get occasionally beat up in B plots on *Victorious*, but to see her take it on the chin from the genuinely mean-spirited Sam in the main plot of nearly every episode got pretty rough,' it declared.

There had been enough drama off – and on – screen for Ariana: she wanted to move into pop music. 'I really want to be a recording artist, it's what I've wanted to do my whole life,' she said at the time. 'Music is my passion and it drives this whole career … The community theater was doing musicals so I kind of started acting with that. I definitely want to be a recording artist. Like 24/7 there's music going on in my head, which is kind of distracting! I love music.'

'I hate acting,' she told *Rolling Stone*. 'It's fun, but music has always been first and foremost with me.' But it had made her famous – an idol for tweens who boasted 15 million Twitter followers. And at least her acting in *Victorious* gave her the chance to record her first track on an official album. On the album, *Victorious: Music from the Hit TV Show*, she sang on 'Give It Up', alongside Elizabeth Gillies. The album was released on 2 August 2011 by Nick Records, in association with Sony Music Entertainment. It reached number five on the *Billboard* 200. With this confidence under her belt, Ariana began to film herself performing covers of songs of famous artists, and uploading the videos on to YouTube.

It was a sharp move – and one that had previously propelled Justin Bieber to fame. The Canadian started his YouTube channel not out of ambition as much as convenience. After his mother Pattie filmed him singing at a local talent contest, she thought of ways she could share the video with geographically distant relatives. The answer suddenly came to her: YouTube was the perfect answer! All she had to do was upload the videos on to the website and then simply email links to anyone interested in watching them. 'I put my singing videos from the competition on YouTube so that my friends and family could watch them,' Bieber remembered. 'But it turned out that other people liked them,' he added.

Justin found that his videos were perfect for YouTube. As well as his fine voice and cute looks, the 'homemade' style of the videos he continued to upload made them all the more compelling for the general public. As the 'hit counter' for his videos shot upwards, Biebs began to receive a deluge of positive feedback from people who had watched and loved them. He was building quite an online fan base. As we shall see, his offerings were eventually watched by the man who would manage him, and would subsequently also manage Ariana. So there is a nice congruence to the fact that Ariana, too, took the YouTube route.

One of the first of her videos was a cover of British superstar Adele's hit 'Rolling in the Deep'. It's an impressive a cappella rendition, if at times a little showy.

As with many young vocalists who aspire to follow in the stylistic footsteps of the people they admire, she tended to focus a little too much on showcasing her vocal range, rather than just performing the song as best she could. Other artists she attempted covers of in this time were Whitney Houston and Mariah Carey.

YouTube proved a wise and successful route for Ariana. This was how she was discovered: a friend of Republic Records' chairman and chief executive Monte Lipman sent him YouTube videos of Ariana covering Whitney Houston and Mariah Carey. Monte's brother, Avery, president and chief operating officer of the record company, felt that there was an element of fate behind how Ariana and the label came together. 'You could look at an Ariana Grande, before her records even came out, and see the passion she inspired. There's a lot of noise out there, but if you know what you're looking for, it shows itself.'

Later, Ariana returned to the stage for a production called *A Snow White Christmas* at the Pasadena Playhouse in California. A reviewer for the *Los Angeles Times* wrote that Ariana, as Snow White, was cheered by the audience for her performance, which he described as 'unaffected and soaring of vocals'. David C. Nichols concluded that the production was 'all harmless fun', though he complained that 'the jokes grow sophomoric, even fairy tales require a measure of actual threat for their happy endings to fully register'.

Asked later by Nichols if she felt she had missed anything important with her fledgling fame, Ariana said: 'You know, maybe prom and homecoming, but I wouldn't have been much fun at them anyway because I'm not really a party girl.' She added that as 'boring' as it sounds, she 'probably would have just stayed home and read *Harry Potter*'. In fact, she was also likely to have stayed home and studied spirituality, because Ariana was about to make a big decision that would change her life in deep ways.

CHAPTER FOUR

A CHANGE OF FAITH

In 2014, Ariana made a significant, life-altering decision about her approach to spirituality. The decision would involve leaving one path and adopting a new one – a more mystical one. Like many Americans with Italian roots Ariana had been brought up a Roman Catholic, but several aspects of the Christian faith's teachings – and one in particular – increasingly troubled her, nagging away at her conscience on a daily basis.

Mainstream Catholicism is strictly disapproving of homosexuality, and the more Ariana thought about this fact, the more she felt that she could not reconcile this aspect of the faith with her love for her elder half-brother Frankie, who is openly gay. Even without Frankie's presence in her life, this might have upset her values of equality and modernity. However, thinking of

Frankie focused her mind. He had received a judgement that went beyond the official Catholic position, which judges only the acts, rather than the committer of the acts. 'When my brother was told that God didn't love him I was like, "OK, that's not cool",' she said in the *Sunday Telegraph*. Such loyalty: she is just the sort of sister any boy should be lucky enough to have. She was not about to overlook the prejudice her brother was facing. She had no intention of shrugging it off, just because it did not affect her directly.

Indeed, this was not the only issue she had with the Church. Ariana also found there were other aspects of Catholicism that clashed with her life. It just stopped feeling like the right fit for her, despite her ancestral connection with the religion. 'I was born Roman Catholic,' she said, 'but I lost faith when the Pope decided to tell me everything I loved and believed in was wrong.'

Bizarrely, she thought that these included a comment she believes the Catholic Church – but not the Pope himself – had reportedly made about her favourite cartoon. She told the *Daily Telegraph*, '[The Church] said Spongebob Squarepants is gay and he's a sinner and he should burn in hell. And *Harry Potter* was a sin. And working women. I was like "Enough! First the gays, then Spongebob and now *Harry Potter*? Get out my house!" I was not having it. And the working woman thing? It was a moment for me. I needed something else to believe in.'

However, she did not want to leave religion and spirituality behind entirely. So she thought she would find a new path to the same destination. When she and Frankie heard that a Kabbalah centre was being opened in Florida, they decided to go along and see what they found behind its doors. After hearing about other people's rewarding experiences with Kabbalah they were not sure what they would find but they felt it was worth a go – and they were pleased that they did. 'We both checked it out and really had a connection with it,' Ariana said. Her nature as a spiritual truth-seeker and the courage of her walk were both being rewarded. Rather than blindly sticking with the tradition she was born into, she looked around and tried to find one that fitted.

But what is Kabbalah? It is a mystical branch, or offshoot, of Judaism, the Jewish faith. It is, therefore, the overall 'umbrella' term for Jewish mysticism. According to the website of the Kabbalah Center, the organization that Ariana first got involved with: 'Kabbalah is an ancient wisdom that provides practical tools for creating joy and lasting fulfillment. It's an incredible system of technology that will completely change the way you look at your world.'

As Ari discovered, Kabbalah's main book is called the Zohar, an epic, dense and frequently puzzling tome that has thrilled and bamboozled readers in equal measure for centuries. As she entered Kabbalah, the Zohar became Ariana's new go-to book. Part of the wonder of it is that it is really several books in one. It is a mystical commentary on the Torah (the Jewish holy book), but it also reads like a mystical novel about a group of rabbis, who wander around the hills of Galilee in northern Israel, discussing life, the universe and everything. They encounter interesting characters on the way, and it feels that every story is carefully measured to provide a metaphor for life. In one story, a village idiot is revealed to be a deep and intelligent thinker.

Several aspects of the Zohar have caused controversy within mainstream religion. For instance, it uses erotic imagery, suggesting that God has a male and female aspect, and it is only when mankind performs good deeds on earth, that these two aspects are sufficiently aroused to come together into one. This more feminist take on godliness was something that will have appealed to Ariana.

Also, although the Zohar uses the Bible as a springboard for the imagination, it also retranslates many of the key passages of the Bible, making them mean something quite different. The first five words of the Bible read: 'In the beginning, God created ...' But the Zohar even turns this on its head. It insists on interpreting the first Hebrew words in their precise order, which would make it read: 'With beginning, it created God.' So God has gone from the subject of the sentence to the object. This is more than a mere linguistic change; it is, for some mainstream Jews and Christians, tantamount to blasphemy.

Although the Zohar's approach has shaken up mainstream faith, that fact is unlikely to have troubled Ariana as she began to investigate Kabbalah. In fact, it is easy to see how this aspect of the belief system will have been right up her street. She likes inventive, ground-breaking approaches. The book, and Kabbalah itself, is full of puns, parables and paradoxes. It must have felt a breath of fresh air to Ariana, as she wrenched herself away from the familiarity of Catholicism. She might also have found a pleasant serendipity in the fact that one of the Kabbalah's leading historical luminaries, Isaac Luria, was nicknamed 'the Ari'.

Kabbalah has become synonymous in the media with celebrity members, thanks to the many famous followers it has attracted in recent years. The most famous of all is one of Ariana's childhood heroes, Madonna, who became enthusiastically involved in the faith, right down to wearing its iconic red string on her wrist. Her involvement coincided with Kabbalah's ascendancy. The *Los Angeles Times* has reported that in 1998, the year after Madonna went public with her ties to Kabbalah, the Kabbalah Center had $20 million in assets. By 2009, those assets had grown to $260 million.

In many ways, Madonna was an unintended trailblazer for Ariana. She drew out the shock the public would feel over a celebrity joining such a movement. 'When the world discovered I was studying Kabbalah, I was accused of joining a cult,' Madonna said on Facebook. 'I was accused of being brainwashed. Of giving away all my money. I was accused of all sorts of crazy things.'

This meant that by the time Ariana joined up, the idea of celebrities in Kabbalah was regarded more casually. As Madonna has explained, it is a harmless pursuit. 'I wasn't hurting anybody,' she told *Harper's Bazaar*. 'Just going to class, taking notes in my spiral notebook, contemplating my future. I was actually trying to become a better person.'

Other famous people who have reportedly taken an interest in Kabbalah include Britney Spears, Roseanne Barr, Sandra Bernhard and Ashton Kutcher. Also, Demi Moore, Elizabeth Taylor, Paris Hilton and Lindsay Lohan are said to have taken refuge under the umbrella of its teachings at times. So it has a strong connection with the show-business world, the depth of which perhaps even its ancient sages would have been unable to foresee.

How would it have been for Ariana, a famous face, when she began to attend Kabbalah events? An insight into this can be drawn from the description of how Madonna is regarded when she shows up at the London Kabbalah Centre. A director there told the *Guardian*: 'She'll walk into a class or event and sit next to a random person – who might text a friend to say, "Guess who's sitting next to me?" But everyone here is respectful.'

Ariana later told *Billboard* that sharing a belief system with her hero, Madonna, gave her a new flush of empathy. 'As a fellow Kabbalist, I know how hard it is to exercise those tools in your everyday life,' says Grande. 'Especially in a world where everything is so egocentric and all you do is talk about yourself and promote yourself.'

As for Ariana herself, she has also done some of her learning in private. She has written on Twitter about her Skype sessions with her Kabbalah teacher, Ruthie. However, Ariana thus far has been rather reticent to discuss her involvement with Kabbalah in any depth. She did, however, tell the *Sunday Telegraph* magazine how her life changed when she first walked through the doors. 'Since then, my life has unfolded in a really beautiful way, and I think that it has a lot to do with the tools I've learned through Kabbalah, I really do,' she said.

Asked to explain what the tools are, she said: 'You have to watch your intentions, make sure you're not giving in to your ego. You have to numb your reactive state. You have the power to change your reality.' Although her interviewer described Ariana's mood as 'bashful' when the topic had come up, she did add more meat to the bone. 'You have to take a second and breathe and reassess how you want to approach or react to a situation or approach an obstacle, or deal with a negative person in your space,' she said. 'That takes a lot of self-control and practice and, I guess, willpower.'

It is hoped that one day she will feel comfortable to elaborate on what Kabbalah has done for her.

The ideas that Ariana is pointing to include the central Kabbalah Center teaching that you get from life what you put in. If you do a good deed, a good deed will be done to you. If you do something unpleasant, that, too, will come back to you. It is a simple teaching but one that, when followed closely, can change someone's every action throughout the day. The challenging part comes when the follower is forced to consider whether anything bad that happens to them, or their loved ones, is in some sense 'deserved'.

Catholicism's position on homosexuality could have become something that divided Ariana and Frankie. Instead, through their exploration of Kabbalah, it seems to have become the springboard for them coming closer together. They went on a spiritual journey together – not unlike the rabbis in the Zohar, one could say – and found fulfilment.

Will Ariana's interest in Kabbalah begin to directly affect her musical material? There are precedents. Several of Madonna's songs are believed to relate to Kabbalah, including 'Isaac', which is thought to be about the key Kabbalistic figure Isaac Luria and features on her album *Confessions on a Dance Floor*. It is also thought that the track 'Ray of Light' was influenced to a degree by Kabbalah teachings.

Ariana is more than open to the idea of collaboration

with Madonna. 'Oh my God, my heart would stop,' she gushed when *Billboard* suggested such a hook-up. 'She is strength, she is freedom, she is wisdom beyond anybody's comprehension.' Although Madonna's long-standing connection with Kabbalah has, to an extent, normalized the faith in society's eyes, some hardliners are still terrified by it. Accordingly, Ariana has, like Madonna, attracted criticism from some quarters for her journey into Kabbalah. 'She has embraced ... a satanic cult religion,' said Maryland pastor David Whitney. 'It's called Kabbalah, it is a Jewish cult belief system that is the opposite, in a sense, of our Christian faith.'

From Catholic child to Kabbalah student, accused of promoting a 'satanic cult', Ariana's spiritual journey to date had indeed been astonishing. In 2010, looking back over her career to date, she said that the greatest aspect of it was 'being able to give back'. As she explained in the *Mirror*: 'I'm able to do everything I've wanted to do at such an early age and so kids look up to me. I get to be a role model, and being a good role model is definitely one of the best parts of this.' Given the importance of selflessness and charity in the teachings of the Kabbalah, it was clear that she was absorbing this well.

By this stage, Ariana had released her first single, so let's get back to the music ...

CHAPTER FIVE

A MUSICAL DEBUT

Ariana's position at the time she released her first track was atypical for a debut act, about to be launched by their label. She was not an unknown because she had acted on Broadway and national television, and had a burgeoning YouTube following. Neither, though, was she releasing her first single as a hugely famous face, as would be the case if she had gone through the reality television, talent show route.

As Republic Records' Monte Lipman put it on the website HITS Daily Double: 'She clearly was having a certain level of success in the TV space and Nickelodeon. She had never put a record out, but she had created this incredible following in the social space, doing covers and little videos and really engaging with her fans. When you talk about that creative leap of faith, what we saw, first and foremost, was an extraordinary talent. We started thinking, "If we find a way to partner with this young lady, what's the strategy?" All these different factors come into place.'

They came into place on 12 December 2011, when she released the single 'Put Your Hearts Up', a pop song aimed at the hearts of her young *Victorious* audience. Although it is a song from which she has since distanced herself, it has many merits, not least in understanding the trajectory of her career. Inspired by the doo-wop sounds of the 1950s and 1960s, the lyrics of 'Put Your Hearts Up' were a call to arms for a generation. Neon Limelight described her vocal performance on the song as 'Demi-Lovato-meets-Kelly-Clarkson-meets-Mariah-Carey-style' and, during a chat with the same publication, Ariana listed one of those singers as her key inspiration.

'I love Mariah Carey. She is literally my favorite human being on the planet,' she said. 'And of course Whitney [Houston] as well. As far as vocal influences go, Whitney and Mariah pretty much cover it. I love Fergie as well. She's just so fun and passionate. I love that she raps as well. Like, she has a fantastic voice and she can belt Gs and As and she doesn't have to do it all the time. She just has swag and I think that's really cool.'

This message of changing the world for the better was an enormously positive one for her burgeoning young fan base to hear. They responded with excitement:

#BuyPutYourHeartsUp quickly became the number-one trending topic worldwide on Twitter. The fans were so animated because, thanks to Ariana's online activity, they felt involved. A few days before the single's release she had popped up on Twitter to ask fans which of four possible cover-art options they thought should be chosen for the single. Then it was time for the release: it premiered on 9 December 2011 on *On Air With Ryan Seacrest*, the former presenter of *American Idol* and mainstay of the American pop media. The song was available for digital download through iTunes three days later.

At the time, Ariana said of the new single: 'It's a song that I hope inspires people to put their hearts up and that even the smallest acts of kindness can make the world a better place.' In a more clinical moment, she also told ryanseacreast.com the track was selected as her debut single because it was the 'best option for a newcomer, most commercial'. She added that it screams 'newbie coming to town'.

But when it came to the shooting of the song's promotional video, which kicked off on 23 November 2011, a lot of the fun went out of the experience from Ariana's point of view. In an interview with *Bestseller* magazine, she said the editing had been 'quite an adventure' because it was her first time shooting a music video and she was nervous and 'we were losing light as the day was going on'. Hinting at discord between her and the crew, she added: 'It's hard because sometimes the director wants to focus more on the continuity and the storyline, and I just want to focus on the performance and the dancing and the beauty of it, and not work on color correction, CGI, and silly effects and stuff. They're like "you have to work on the subtext". Like, no.'

Perhaps a large part of her disdain for the process came from simple nerves as she transitioned from tween sitcom to music video. After all, she said that being alone in front of the camera for the first time 'was a big adjustment'. She explained: 'Whenever I was on camera [before], I was always with my friends from the show. It was just me and my friends goofing around, but this was just me. And I was like oh my God! It was kind of scary at first, but I loved it and I got used to it.' By the end of it, she said, she felt like her childhood hero, Audrey Hepburn.

Ariana had been on the set of music videos before, as a dancer or extra, at which she had noticed that some of the dancers were very blasé about the experience. They told her: 'I don't wanna be here, I wanna go home.' But when it came to shooting the video for 'Put Your Hearts Up', it was a different story. 'Everyone was really excited to be there,' she told Neon Limelight. 'Everyone was so excited. And when we weren't shooting, we were literally on the Universal lot having a photoshoot and doing silly things.'

When she saw the final product, she loved it so

much that she quickly had not just one favourite part, but 'like a million favorite parts'! She said she loved the beginning 'because I get to free a little cartoon butterfly on a balcony, and it's really cute and girly and everything I could hope for'. The bridge was also another favourite part for her, 'because it's a *Singin' in the Rain* homage and I love old movies so much'. She added: 'It's really cute.'

However, reflecting on the video a few years later, she told a different story. 'It was geared toward kids and felt so inauthentic and fake,' she sniffed, during a chat with *Rolling Stone* magazine. 'That was the worst moment of my life. For the video, they gave me a bad spray tan and put me in a princess dress and had me frolic around the street. The whole thing was straight out of hell. I still have nightmares about it, and I made them hide it on my Vevo page.'

She also told Zach Sang and the Gang that the experience felt to her the same as looking back on old social media posts and cringing hard. 'That's like scrolling too far back on Facebook, and you're like, "oh s**t!"' she said. But the single still fared well: it was later certified gold by the Recording Industry Association of America (RIAA).

'Put Your Hearts Up' was originally meant to be the lead single for Ariana's debut album. Perhaps unsurprisingly, given her dislike for the song, it was subsequently replaced in that position by 'The Way', which dropped on 25 March 2013. She had spent the weeks leading up to the release working her fans into a lather on Twitter. On 5 March she tweeted about 'The Way', telling her fans its release was forthcoming. Then on 13 March she formally confirmed the release date. Three days after that, she uploaded a teaser trail for the track on to YouTube and followed up with another teaser on 21 March, just forty-eight hours before the single's release.

The song would create a legal headache for Ariana and her team when the British independent publisher Minder Music alleged it infringed their copyright. The action claimed that in 'The Way' she had interpolated elements of Minder's composition 'Troglodyte', originally recorded by The Jimmy Castor Bunch. These sorts of suits are far from unheard of in pop, and in 2015 it was announced that the matter had been settled. Details of the settlement remained under wraps, but Minder's MD John Fogarty told Music Business Worldwide: 'We have arrived at an amicable solution which was to everybody's satisfaction'.

Then came the promotional tour, during which she visited a host of radio stations – including Y-100 Miami and 93.3 FM – for interviews and spins of the track. She also rolled up on the *Elvis Duran and the Morning Show* and attended a release party thrown by the Z100 station, where she spoke about her career. After other appearances, 'The Way' debuted once again on *On Air with Ryan Seacrest*.

The critics were keen. 'We're as guilty as anyone of drawing lazy comparisons between artists and songs, but in the case of Ariana's new single, likening it to Mariah Carey feels particularly valid because, well, it really sounds like a Mariah Carey song,' wrote Robert Copsey of Digital Spy. Nick Catucci of *Rolling Stone* drew a similar comparison, writing that Ariana is 'more flirty than freaky, but her Mariah-esque vocals verge on ecstatic'. MTV said the song suggested Ariana 'may very well be the hottest pop newcomer in the game'.

With her fame and stature soaring, Ariana used it to a positive and giving end when she joined *Seventeen* magazine's 'Delete Digital Drama' campaign, which targeted cyberbullying. Lending her support, Ariana said cyberbullies 'are just people who don't know what to do with themselves. They're bored with their own lives so they pick on other people. They bully because they're jealous or insecure.' She also offered a practical tip for anyone who was upset by online bullying when she added: 'I can't stress to you enough how much I can relate to teens being cyberbullied. Something that helps me is looking at old videos of me and my friends from middle school, or videos of my family. I love watching funny videos of my favorite people – it really cheers me up.'

She returned to the acting field briefly, to voice the title role in the English dub of the Spanish-language animated film *Snowflake the White Gorilla*, but it was in music where her heart lay, so it was a nice end to the year for her when she was named as one of *Billboard*'s '21 under 21 – music's hottest minors' for 2013. Above her were Miley Cyrus, Justin Bieber and One Direction. On her tail were Earl Sweatshirt and Lorde.

This was also a nice way to go into the release of her debut album – a huge step for Ariana, who had dreamed for so long of releasing an album, and worked so hard to make it happen. She would bring a new face to her team for the release time. A pop Svengali who was responsible for launching the career of the twenty-first century's hottest male pop act. He had already discovered and guided the career of pop star Justin Bieber. In doing so, he became a star himself – his name was Scooter Braun.

The grandchild of Holocaust survivors and once a teenage party promoter in Atlanta, Scooter became one of the show-business industry's hottest rising stars when he shot to fame simultaneously with his first major talent – Justin Bieber. So who is he? Scott 'Scooter' Braun was born in Greenwich, Connecticut in 1982, a whole eleven years before Ariana was born. Like Ariana, Scooter showed an enterprising streak early on in his life. Looking back on his childhood, he said, 'I was a little bit rebellious and I was very social, but I was also a homebody.' He adds that he has not really changed.

This anecdote feels significant. 'I remember when I was a kid and the teacher thought I was cheating because I had the answer on the math test, but when she looked at my work it didn't make any sense to her, he told Papermag. 'And I said, "No, I didn't [cheat], let me show you," and I showed her, like, this roundabout way that I solved the equation. And she said, "Why would you ever do it like that?" and I said, "Why wouldn't I?" I've always wanted to do things the way I want to do them.'

A successful, popular pupil at school, Scooter was voted class president. Later, during his first year at university – he attended Emory University in Atlanta – he started his first ever business. He said he wanted to earn his own money so he was not dependent on his parents for handouts. As well as a stamina for hard work, he had something else very valuable: the knack to spot the right opportunity and seize it. During his college years, he noticed that an Atlanta nightclub – called Paradox – was struggling to pull any clubbers through its doors on Thursday evenings. So he arranged a Thursday evening bash there on the proviso that while the club took all the profits from drinks, he would pocket all the profits from the entry fees. Over a thousand people arrived and Braun cashed in big time. He arranged further Thursday evening parties and was soon building himself quite a reputation as a party organizer – and this would take him up the ladder.

After they had met at a nightclub, hip-hop star Ludacris contacted Braun and asked him to organize parties for him as he toured around America alongside Eminem. Braun took the challenge on and arranged successful bashes in New York, Miami, Atlanta, Tampa and Hartford. Quite remarkable: Braun was still not even out of his teens but he was already proving to be a smart businessman. He left university early, which initially disappointed his father, but it is safe to say that he has since rather vindicated his decision. His reputation spread and he went on to arrange social events for other famous people – and also began networking in the music world.

Then came a huge turning point that led to a path that changed everything. One day he received a phone call from a music producer called Jermaine Dupri. Having produced hit albums for Mariah Carey and Usher, Dupri was a big figure in the music industry, and he was so impressed with Braun's track record that he hired him to his record label, So So Def Recordings. Based in Atlanta, Georgia it specialized in hip-hop, soul and other black music.

Braun soared within the organization and quickly assumed the impressive job title of executive director of marketing. Among his fellow workers Braun had a less formal but equally positive title: 'Hustla', a streetwise spelling of the word 'hustler'. He was delighted to be called this, as to him 'a hustla is somebody that doesn't take no for an answer; somebody who had a vision and a goal and works to realize it; somebody who works his [butt] off to make it happen'. He soon became a man who played the part of the guy he was grafting to become. He drove a flash purple Mercedes CLK 320 and arranged parties involving A-list celebrities, including the likes of Britney Spears, and he rubbed shoulders with hip-hop royalty including Kanye West, whom he would later manage.

Ariana's future boss has shown he had plenty of vision and was a mercilessly hard worker. He also had balls. In 2004, at the age of twenty-three, he took the brave step of leaving So So Def because he wanted to form his own company, which he called SB Projects. It would be a chance for him to shape his own vision, an entertainment and promotion company with a broad church of projects and ambitions. In doing so, it rather reflected Braun himself who has always had multiple things on the go at once, so much so that a friend of his once admitted that even he could not quite keep up with Braun's ventures.

Something that many people who know Braun well seem to agree on is that he deserves every bit of his success. He was about to take an already highly successful career to dizzying new heights and a young Canadian boy would prove to be the vehicle for that trip.

Soon after he formed his own company, Braun took some time off to go and watch a basketball game. As ever with Braun, even when safely away from the office, he found it hard to entirely switch off from work. He lives for success and his head is always buzzing with ideas and dreams. As he was chatting at the game with Ludacris' manager Chaka Zulu, Braun outlined his ambitions for the immediate future. The first was to launch the next big white rap artist. He also explained that he wanted to sign a girl band and a boy singer who 'could do it like Michael Jackson – sing songs that adults would appreciate and be reminded of the innocence they once felt about love'.

These were lofty ambitions – but, being Scooter Braun, he quickly pulled them off. In fact, he discovered his white rapper within weeks, when he signed MC Asher Roth, who quickly had a hit with 'I Love College'. Roth's debut album was a top five hit in America. As for Braun's next Michael Jackson hope, that huge ambition was met while he was browsing the Internet one evening. Expanding on what he was looking for, Braun told the *Washington Post*: 'I wanted someone who was like Michael. Someone who captivated not only kids, but adults, too.' As he stumbled on his first video of a kid called Justin Bieber, Braun thought he had found just that. Indeed, he was so excited, he thought he had struck gold.

It was, so the legend goes at least, entirely by chance that Braun first came across Justin's online presence. 'I was consulting for an act that [singer, songwriter, producer] Akon had in a production deal and I was looking at his YouTube videos,' Braun told *Time* magazine. He went on to explain that it was the 'Related Videos' function of YouTube that took him to Justin.

'The kid was singing Aretha Franklin's "Respect", and there was a related video of Justin singing the same song. I clicked on it thinking it was the same kid and realized that the twenty-year-old I was watching was now twelve.' His reaction on watching Justin's performance of 'Respect' – taken from the Stratford Star singing competition held in Justin's home town – was one of enormous excitement. Not just emotionally, but physically too. 'It was such raw talent, my gut just went wild,' Braun said. Ever the comic, he added: 'Maybe I shouldn't tell people I watched videos of Justin Bieber in the middle of the night.'

Yet it was watching those videos that changed Braun's life, as the cute Canadian kid they featured went on to become one of the modern era's most successful pop talents. It all began when Braun tracked down Bieber's mother Pattie and, during an epic phone call, tried to convince her to let him guide her thirteen-year-old son to fame. Pattie remembered praying, 'God, I gave him to you. You could send me a Christian man, a Christian label!' and, 'God, you don't want this Jewish kid to be Justin's man, do you?' However, she eventually decided to go with Braun.

It proved a wise decision. Over the ten years since Braun's phone call, Bieber has become a pop legend. All this has made him rich: according to *Forbes* magazine, Biebs earned $56 million (£43.5 million) in 2016 alone, with his overall net worth being listed as $225 million

(£175 million). He has won eight Guinness World Records.

All that was guided by Braun. So what is the philosophy he brings to clients, including Ariana? *Forbes* magazine reported that Braun always wants to know one hing before becoming involved in a new venture: Did you burn the ships? In 2016, *Forbes* reported a story that illustrates this well. When a friend called Tom McLeod came to Braun asking for investment, Braun explained that when they landed on emeny shores, the ancient Greeks used to burn their own ships. For Braun, this was a symbolic practice and one that he wanted his friend to follow. So, in answer to the pitch, he told McLeod: 'If we are going to do this, I need to know you're going to burn the ships. There is no turning back, there is no, "Hey, it's getting tough now. It's not really working out. I'm going to fold and try something else." If this is you're [going to] burn the ships, that's a different story.' McLeod eventually got back in touch, said he was indeed going to burn the ships, and he secured Braun's backing.

Another long-standing philosophy of Ariana's boss was that he 'always had this entrepreneurial spirit … and never wants to be limited by anything.' Finally, Braun accepted one that came from his inspiration, producer, film studio executive and philanthropist David Geffen. Geffen told Braun: 'You know, in a hundred years no one's going to remember me, so they sure as hell won't remember you, so don't have an ego.'

Braun has had his challenges, some of which may have come in useful when he managed Ariana, whose career trajectory has thrown up several dramas and crises. He admitted that the period during which Justin Bieber went off the rails was very hard. In an interview with *Teen Vogue* he added: 'You know, I love that kid, and I had never been through anything like that before with someone. And for a year and a half, I felt like a failure. Every single day was a battle. That was the hardest moment in my career, because it was also very personal. I learned a lot about life, about success, about people. And I'm really proud that he came out on the other side, and I'm really proud of the people on our team – we were all really like family [to] him. And no one gave up, no one budged.'

The final word on Braun for now must come in the form of his response to Geffen's quip above. 'Because when I die, I die. I'm not here to see if they remember my name. But I want to leave an impact on the world that is worthwhile, that's significant and makes a difference. And I want to close my eyes on that last day of life and know I did that.'

Part of the impact he will leave on the world will be his guidance of Ariana's dramatic ascendancy to fame. One of the first milestones he was on the books for was the release of her debut album – *Yours Truly* – released on 3 September 2013 by Republic Records. The album is rich with R&B. Indeed, Ariana herself said that the opening half of the collection was a 'throwback' to the

R&B of the 1990s – a precocious statement from an artist of her age. However, in a separate conversation she also trailed it as originating from music from even further back, describing it as '50s, 60s doo-wop-inspired'. She claimed more originality for the material that makes up the second half of the album, telling MTV it is 'very unique and very special that I've sort of written'.

Ariana co-wrote six of the tracks. She was at pains to emphasize that she had not been a pop puppet, passively allowing others to direct and shape the album, before releasing it as her work. 'I got to be heavily creatively involved,' she said. 'I was in charge on everything, which was really exciting for me and I'm so happy.' Speaking to *Elle*, she agreed with their suggestion that she was a 'studio rat'. She said of working in the studio: 'If I could, I would not do anything else. I'd just be in the studio for my whole life. I would never go to parties, events, and red carpets … I just want to make music.'

It had been an epic process. She told *Complex* magazine that she worked on the album for three years, adding: 'I was actually doing it while *Victorious* was going on the whole time … so I've been waiting forever to finally be able to just do this. It was an easy transition for me because I was open to it. It wasn't "Oh, I don't want to work with these people. I want to write my own stuff." It was like, "This is cool because they're the best in the business, and they know what they're doing. They love the sound that I love, and we can do this together."'

Asked on the eve of its release what her fans could expect from it, Ariana painted with words a portrait of a highly personal work. 'It's like a direct ... you know, it's like it used to be pages from my diary, instead of keeping diary, I would write songs about what was happening in my life. So it's really personal.'

Let's examine this really personal collection, song by song. It begins with 'Honeymoon Avenue'. For a pop star to record such a long track is daring enough – to open an album with an epic is braver still. Yet it works: *Billboard* loved its 'pinpoint production, sleek beats ... and commanding vocals', while online magazine *Pitchfork* describes her delivery as 'smoky, world-weary and featherweight all at once'. She said it 'was one of the first songs I ever recorded for my album and it was one of my last', going on to explain that she and the team completely rearranged the production and re-recorded it.

'Baby I' comes next – a track that has been compared by some to the work of pop princess Britney Spears. It was written by the trio of Kenneth 'Babyface' Edmonds, Antonio Dixon and Patrick 'J. Que' Smith. Musically, its uptempo beat is straight from the 1990s textbook, and all the better for it. But it is the lyrics that touch the heart of the listener. It covers the dilemma many feel when they are unable to express their deep feelings of love and devotion for a partner. Many have felt as 'tongue-tied' as Ariana declares herself to be in the song.

'Baby I' was originally written for Beyonce – and you can hear it in the brassy style. 'I loved the song just because it feels a lot like [the Broadway musical] *Dreamgirls* to me,' said Ariana in *Complex* magazine. 'It's so glamorous and I love the song so much and I feel like it shows off my musicality more than "The Way" did – vocally and just the song itself is such a statement and that's what I love about it. "Baby I" is special in the way it's just musical.'

On the third track, 'Right There', the album's first guest appears, in the shape of Big Sean. It's a full-on love song with a promise of an eternity together. Ariana sings about how different her love is from others, how he listens. Later, Big Sean takes the reins with characteristic sass and confidence. The two tones – Ariana, all devoted and starry-eyed, Big Sean bursting with self-assurance – make for a fine dynamic.

'Tattooed Heart' takes the sound back several decades. During interviews, Ariana said that Amy Winehouse had influenced her during the making of *Yours Truly*. This 1950s-flavoured track shows that influence – one can easily hear Winehouse singing such a song. It is a touching and emotional tune, which sees Ariana showcase her vocal pipes to full effect. The lyrics, which again are bursting with devotion, tie in with the album's titular theme of sincere love.

Speaking of which – next up comes 'Lovin' It', on which the tempo paces up but the theme remains much the same. Here, she once again sings of her fulsome devotion. Here, it is an unexpected love, which started with a crush but then became everything. *Billboard* said this was a 'transitional' track that featured Ariana sounding 'giddy while tossing off romantic declarations both sweet and direct'.

'Please allow "Piano" to lay waste to everything else on your favorite playlist,' said *Billboard* of track six on *Yours Truly*. A work of power and authority, it is, wrote Jason Lipshutz, a 'pristine, rollicking love song' with 'sonic daring' and a 'percolating verse' which 'slides' into the 'assured groove of the chorus'. A simpler way of describing it might be to say that it is Ariana's Katy Perry moment.

'Daydreamin'' is one of the album's gentler efforts – described by Pitchfork as *Grease*-calibre cheese. Late in, the song takes on a new life, with gorgeous harmonies. But it is with 'The Way' that the album leaps back into life. We explored this track earlier in the chapter. However, its place in the album is important. As *Billboard* puts it, 'Harmony Samuels' breezy arrangement (built around a Big Pun's sample) and Mac Miller's playful flow cannot overshadow the lightness of Grande's forceful vocal delivery'.

Some songs are growers – tracks that take repeated spins before they grab the listener. 'You'll Never Know' is not one of them: it has an immediate appeal that grabs you and does not let go until it's finished. It drew praise from critics for its 'squelching beat'. Also worth noting is that it departs from the happy tone of much of what precedes it on the album. Here, Ariana is sassy, telling a guy that he messed up.

Then comes another guest artist, for the emotional ballad 'Almost Is Never Enough'. Here, she is joined by Nathan Sykes of British boy band The Wanted, whose US affairs were managed by Scooter Braun. Although this song, too, is a world apart from the happy loving tone of the earlier tracks, here it is not sass but sadness that dominates. The pianist sets a potent atmosphere of regret and Ariana's vocals are mature and resigned. Sykes, too, sings beyond his years, with a soulful tone. However, their joint vocals do not work as well as their separate deliveries.

By now, the album is due a change of pace and tone. Track eleven, 'Popular Song', delivers just that – and then some. With Lebanese/English singer-songwriter Mika alongside her, Ariana pumps out three minutes and twenty seconds of pure fun. With plenty of guitar and more than a few handclaps, the production provides an updated cover of the 'Popular' track from the hit musical *Wicked*. It is a bouncy and catchy effort – the listener can almost feel the fun that Ariana must have had while recording it.

The album is nearly at its end – but before it closes comes 'Better Left Unsaid'. Here, Ariana throws in a plot twist, with a lively club song, which, as *Billboard* put it, 'quickly strides away from [its] demure beginning to

Above: Ariana on stage in 2008, during the curtain call for the opening night of the musical *13*, her Broadway debut.

Below: The cast of *13* at the premiere, with Ariana kneeling centre front.

Above: Ariana and her brother, Frankie, attending the 'Holiday of Hope' tree lighting celebration in November 2009.

Left: Ariana at the Los Angeles premiere of *The Lovely Bones* in 2009.

Above: Ariana with her *Victorious* co-stars, 2010.

Below: Ariana with her mother, Joan, and brother, Frankie, attending the third annual Broadway in South Africa Concert in New York, 2010.

Above: Ariana posing with a pumpkin at *Variety*'s fourth annual Power of Youth event in Hollywood, October 2010.

Right: Ariana with her managerial stable-mate Justin Bieber at *Variety*'s fourth annual Power of Youth event in Hollywood, October 2010.

Above: With her grandfather Frank, mother Joan, brother Frankie and grandmother Marjorie at the opening night of the 2011 *Born Yesterday* revival on Broadway, which Frankie produced.

Below: Patti LaBelle duetting with the birthday girl at Ariana's eighteenth birthday extravaganza in New York in 2011.

Above left: Ariana with her mother Joan, who has been a rock to the young singer throughout her career.

Above right: With her much-loved brother Frankie at Macy's Back to School Summer Blow Out concert, New York, 2011.

Left: Ariana with *Sam & Cat* co-star Jennette McCurdy in New York, 2013.

Above: Ariana poses with Katy Perry backstage at the MTV EMAs in Amsterdam, 2013.

Below: Chris Rock's daughter, Zahra, presents Ariana with the Favorite TV Actress Award for her role in *Sam & Cat* at Nickelodeon's twenty-seventh annual Kids' Choice Awards in Los Angeles, 2014.

include pounding synths and DJ calls of "If you wanna party, put your hands up!"' It is a feel-good romp during which Ariana insists that she's gonna say things that she shouldn't. Thus the final trio of songs on *Yours Truly* have moved from mournful ballad, to bubbly pop fun, and then in-your-face club glory. Ariana was laying down a statement there: showing her listeners and fans just what a versatile artist she is.

She was sending a message to the critics, too. How would they regard her work? The *New York Daily News* asked whether twenty-one is 'too young to start looking back', concluding: 'Not for Ariana Grande.' Jim Farber's review continued that the album saw her 'tripping through the scales, while alighting on melodies meant to recall the 1990s glory days of Mariah Carey', whose 'willowy timbre' Ariana shared. He went even further, saying Ariana's songs 'prove far more tuneful than Mariah's interchangeable hits'. He concluded that the album 'proves she can transition to grown-up pop star with something far more substantial than Miley Cyrus has: chops'.

The *Los Angeles Times* said the album was 'charmingly retrograde', going on to say 'it might be the most inviting pop record of 2013, with a bubbly ebullience that makes even its most familiar moves feel fresh'. Mikael Wood concluded that 'there's no discounting Grande's singing', with its 'impressive technical flexibility' that 'captures something true about the intermediate phase she's in right now: a tween queen ageing up, a TV star taking on music, a simpler-times nostalgist peeking around the bend'.

Not all reviewers were so kind, though. Gregory Hicks of *Michigan Daily* complained that the album was dominated by 'unoriginality'. He continued that 'beat usage becomes excessive at times' and that 'Baby, I' 'results in messiness'. Elsewhere, he meowed, the work becomes 'increasingly monotonous'. He denounces Grande as a 'Mariah-Carey ripoff'. Pitchfork's Andrew Ryce said 'songwriting is the album's biggest flaw'.

Thank goodness, then, for online magazine *PopMatters*, which lauds Ariana's 'exceptional voice', with its 'mature timbre and control ... balanced by a young and cute vocal affect', together with 'an impressive amount of emotional control and direction'. Scott Interrante concludes that *Yours Truly* is 'an impressive debut'.

The blogger Random J. Pop had lots of nice things to say, including about Ariana's vocals: 'She can really sing. Really frickin' sing. This is never hidden or downplayed.' Turning to the album itself, they say it is a 'polished debut'. Ultimately concluding, 'There is enough here to leave you wanting to see where Ariana goes next for her follow up.'

Lewis Corner of Digital Spy was also impressed, saying the album's songs 'feel accomplished, polished and vibrant', and that 'as far as pop introductions go, *Yours Truly* is little less than a triumph'. *Billboard*, too, praised her, writing that 'Thankfully, Ariana Grande's debut LP is a surprisingly varied affair by a singer with a devastatingly strong voice. There is a lot to like about *Yours Truly*, and a lot to look forward to in Grande's career.'

For Ariana, the words of the critics were not as important as the response of her fans and the wider public. All the same, any praise she received was welcome. Many artists feel that you can best judge the quality of work not by what a handful of reviewers write, but by how enthusiastically the material is sold. On this basis, she could be pleased. *Yours Truly* shot to number one on the iTunes Store charts in over thirty countries. These included the United States, where it reached the top spot within nineteen minutes of its release. The impressive statistics just kept on coming as she became the the first female artist to have their first album debut at the top of the charts since January 2010.

Charlie Walk, Republic Records' vice president in charge of PR and promotions, who had been given the task of getting the record out there and sold, had put in a good shift for Ariana and the label. 'I give Charlie a tremendous amount of credit because, you know, not even sixty days on the job, he led the campaign with Ariana Grande to deliver a #1-selling single and album,' Monte Lipman told HITS Daily Double. 'He led the charge, and a lot of people would not go into the project thinking, "Hey, let's go for number one; let's hit this thing out of the park right out of the gate.'" Charlie Walk is currently the president of Republic Records, so he has done well out of it. The label was delighted with Walk and thrilled with Ariana. Everything had come together nicely for her debut album, which boded very well for the future.

The youthful demographic of Ariana's fan base saw an interesting ratio in her sales, which were dominated by the digital format. Some 108,000 of her first-week sales were from digital downloads, while *Yours Truly* sold just 30,000 copies through physical sales. It was certified gold in Japan. All in all, then, the album had been a triumphant debut for Ariana. Though it had a somewhat torturous conception, the resultant baby was one of which she could be enormously proud. At her tender age, to release an album *and* be widely compared to Mariah Carey is no mean feat in itself.

Ariana was given a great chance to promote the album when she was invited to join Justin Bieber on tour. She joined the pop prince on his Believe tour for three shows in early August. Following those dates, she set out on her own headlining tour, entitled The Listening Sessions, which kicked off on 13 August 2013 in Silver Spring, Maryland. After that, she played nine cities in the US throughout August, with the jaunt ending on 31 August in Kansas City, Missouri.

In preparation for the dates, she put plenty of time and sweat in. She told *MTV News*, 'I'm rehearsing a lot. I'm working out a lot, trying to get my lungs, my breath support, stronger. I'm training myself to work with in-ear [monitors], which is new for me because I've never worked with in-ears. I've always liked to sing with my natural ear … I'm training my voice to get used to singing every day because I took a long break from singing every single day because I was filming a TV show [Nickelodeon's *Sam & Cat*] so I was sort of not singing as much for a couple weeks … Lots of vocal rest, lots of tea, lots of getting ready.'

She added she was really looking forward to the live dates. 'And I'm helping arrange everything 'cause I'm incredibly anal. So I'm helping arrange the parts for the backup singers, the horns, the violins, the band and everything, 'cause I'm very hands-on when it comes to music. I'm rehearsing a lot. We've been choreographing the whole album, but I'm adding some things that I think my fans will be really happy to see me do.'

The dates that Ariana appeared on Bieber's tour coincided with a racy tabloid storm over a photograph she had posted of her and the Canadian kissing. It was not only the media that got animated about it – Bieber's army of super-possessive fans also had plenty to say. Yet, during an All Access interview on MTV, Ariana herself said: 'I went to meet and greet with my grandparents, because my nonna has a massive crush on Justin Bieber, so I went and our fans … I think they trended #JustinandArianaSelfie or something like that. So I was like, "We have to do this", and Justin was like, "Yeah, let's take a picture".' She continued, 'So, I took my phone and I went like this [gestures selfie] and I was just smiling, and he kissed me on the cheek. I didn't know what to do. I just walked out of the room. I got shy.'

Justin's manager, Scooter Braun, chased after Ariana and tried to persuade her to post the photograph. At first she said she didn't want to because she knew it would cause a storm with Justin's fans but Braun eventually persuaded her and so it ended up posted. As the Beliebers went wild about the story, Ariana responded quickly on Twitter: 'Everyone, girls are allowed to be friends with guys. I'm a lady. Chill out,' successfully defusing what could have been a dangerous ticking time bomb. For, as many people have discovered to their pain, the Belieber army is not one to get on the wrong side of. In both number and dedication, once summoned, it is a powerful militia.

With the crisis averted, Ariana ended the year on a happy and warm note, with a festive EP. Entitled *Christmas Kisses*, it was a collection of Christmas covers, kicking off with 'Last Christmas', moving through 'Love Is Everything' and 'Snow in California', before concluding with 'Santa Baby'. The songs were dropped on a weekly basis, the last track featuring former *Victorious* co-star Liz Gillies. Ariana had trailed the release on Twitter on 6 November, writing: 'I'm releasing new music for Christmas! New song every week as a countdown to the holidays ... Beyond excited to share them w/ U! ... Hope u love the music.'

She did a short promotional stint to help publicize the release, including at the 87th annual Macy's Thanksgiving Day Parade, NBC New York's Rockefeller Center Christmas Tree lighting broadcast and the KIIS-FM Jingle Ball in Los Angeles' Staples Center. It turned out that the fans did, indeed, 'love the music' – and so did the media. Yet over and above the material itself and the reaction to it was the fact that she had been assertive and proud as the album came together. Not for Ariana the role of the unquestioning naïf, allowing the more seasoned industry to impose their vision. She was not about to parrot the 'I'm just grateful to be here' cliché that some young pop acts like to express. Instead, she dug her heels in when needed.

She told *Billboard* that at the heart of her position was that she was 'growing up – I'm almost twenty'. So, she said: 'I'm not going to do anything crazy, but I want to do music that I'm passionate about.' Warming to her theme, she said: 'I'm finally at an age where I can do the music that I grew up loving, which was urban pop, 90s music. I grew up listening to the divas, so I'm very happy to finally do urban pop. I hope that it's received well, and it has been so far.'

Ariana had to fight harder to get her way, because many people she came across tended to assume she was much younger than she was. Perhaps due to her cute looks and petite stature, Ariana found she was often mistaken for someone much younger than she is. The 'Fancy' hit-maker Iggy Azalea pointed to this when she explained in an interview why she had declined the chance to work with Ariana on *Yours Truly*. 'She reached out to me for her first album,' Azalea told Grammy.com. 'And I didn't do it, even though I thought she was amazing, because I thought she was much younger than what she is. When I realized she was so close to my age, I was like – wait you're an adult!'

Soon, Ariana made her realize that she was an adult. She had made a lot of people get used to that idea during the making of *Yours Truly*. She emerged from the process as a bigger star than before – and a stronger, bolder human being. Another way in which people misunderstood her was when they thought her cute face meant she would be a pushover in life. Anyone who made that assumption tended to lose it quickly if they tried to get leverage over her.

Ariana was moving boldly but also speedily – the dust was still settling from her debut album when the second one hit the shelves. And what a step up it was to be. Her work ethic drove her forward. Like many of the best musicians, she was a restless soul, whose greatest fear was to find herself resting on her laurels. Instead, she was keen to drive forward into new tomorrows, with yesterdays soon forgotten. 'As soon as *Yours Truly* debuted at No. 1, I celebrated for an hour, then I was like, "Let's get back to work",' she said.

CHAPTER SIX

THE 'DIFFICULT
SECOND ALBUM'

The music industry generally considers an artist's second work to be the standout challenge of their career – the much-discussed 'difficult second album'. For those artists whose debut was heavily praised and commercially successful, this is a particular worry. The problem here is the expectations create such pressure that they eventually make the superstars buckle. However, from an outsider's perspective these albums can be interesting to observe. What challenges and narratives can we glean from the material and the discussion of it?

The bottom line is that the artist or band have to work that much harder and dig that bit deeper with follow-up albums, because second albums are seen, rightly or wrongly, as a test of whether you're just passing through or are a serious artist who will stick around, and whose work will stand the test of time.

There is also the fact that a debut album will generally have been made more slowly than its successor. Sometimes, the act will have been working on material for album one for several years, whereas for album two there will often be pressure on them to get it out on the shelves in a matter of months, while they remain 'hot'. Also known as the sophomore slump, this trend has been objectively measured. And it is perhaps telling that most Mercury prizes have been awarded to debut, rather than follow-up, efforts.

For Ariana, it was time for work to begin on her follow-up – and she had clear visions and boundaries for it. She said she wanted an 'evolution' in the sound from her first album – and she got it. With more adult themes and a broader, harder range of musical styles and sounds, *My Everything* was a superb knock-on. It was louder, too; and it emerged from an intensive, yet short, gestation period.

The very month of *Yours Truly*'s release, Ariana was already speaking to *Rolling Stone* magazine about the follow-up. 'I've started working on it,' she told them. 'I've come up with a few, two songs already that I want on it. It's an album that I want to do a little bit different.' She added: 'I don't want it to sound like an extension of *Yours Truly*. I want it to sound like an evolution. I want to explore more sounds and experiment a little bit. I have a bunch of ideas I'm very excited about and a lot of stuff cooking.'

The studio work itself kicked off in the autumn of 2013. Although she wanted a new sound, she went with the same producers from her debut: Harmony Samuels and Tommy Brown. She was parked in the studio for several months – it was nearly the summer of 2014 before she finally finished work. She had enjoyed the work. 'It was a very exciting thing for me to all of a sudden have this new mission, to make something as special as *Yours Truly*, and to put my time and effort into something new and something I want to make just as good, if not better.'

It was then that she posed for the photographs for the cover and packaging, going for a simple yet strong cover to match the songs that she felt were so 'strongly themed'. It was also a racier cover than many expected – the teasing, revealing photos were borderline adult in theme. For some of her fans this was a shock but Ariana was adamant that as she grew in years, so would her image have to mature and evolve.

The album itself gets rolling with the aptly titled 'Intro'. Here, it is as if Ariana is merely warming up, vocally jamming, you could say. Yet Ariana can make such an experience sound majestic – and she does. At just one minute and twenty seconds in length, this short song sets a tone for the album very well.

Then the album begins to get really bold – and quickly. 'Problem' is brassy and loud – it's not just in your face, it also grabs you by the ears and refuses to let go. The horn riff is glorious, in the background Big Sean is tantalizing and Ariana is on fire. It is quite a track and bursting with stylish swagger. Ariana co-wrote it with Aussie rapper Iggy Azalea (who was also the featured artist on the track), Savan Kotecha, Ilya and Max Martin. For Ariana, the song is important as it deals with 'the feeling of being absolutely terrified to re-approach a relationship that's gone sour – but you want to more than anything'.

Ariana had wanted to work with Azalea for some time. 'I fell in love with Iggy when I saw this video of her performing "Work" live, and I just thought she was so original and I loved the way she pronounced her words,' Ariana told *Rolling Stone*. 'I thought we would make the perfect girl-power duo for "Problem", so I'm very grateful that she did it with me.'

Swedish songwriter and producer Max Martin has also been a long-term target for Ariana – and for her label. Wendy Goldstein, Grande's A&R rep at Republic, spent two years trying to get Martin involved; finally, when work was about to begin on Grande's album, Martin said he was in. 'He has a young daughter that's a huge Ariana fan,' says Goldstein. 'He said, "I've never seen my daughter excited about someone that I've worked with, and that's really saying something."'

Co-writer Savan Kotecha is a big Martin fan, too. 'He has this Swedish-ness in the back of his mind,' said Kotecha in an interview with *Rolling Stone*. 'He never got caught up in his own hype or being a hotshot producer. He just keeps doing the work.'

As for Kotecha himself, he explained how his lyrical input for this track worked: he was inspired by a woman's lifestyle magazine. 'I keep a list of titles and phrases in my phone that I hear or read from a movie or a magazine,' he said. 'And then, a lot of the times, I build a melody around them. The line "one less problem without you" [on "Problem"] was inspired by something I read in *Cosmopolitan*.'

It is a glorious song – Ariana's sweet vocals form an effective contrast with Iggy's rough-edged rap and the raunchy sax. As Sharon Dastur, an American radio programmer, puts it: 'It has so many layers – Iggy's rap, the beat dropping out, that saxophone, Ariana's voice. It's the biggest buzz song out right now.' Meanwhile, music blog Idolator said it was 'an odd blend of 90s pop and current urban trends but there's no denying that it's catchy'.

However, initially, Ariana had issues with it. 'I loved the idea of it, but the chorus, the whisper was so shocking to me,' she told *Billboard* of the Big Sean section. However, she felt the song gave her a golden opportunity to showcase more of her range – what she described as her 'normal, I'm-not-screaming voice'. She remembers being anxious in the studio. 'I was scared to approach it, because of the whispers,' she told *Rolling Stone*. 'Their objective was to do the opposite of a traditional song structure. The idea was to have a really belt-y verse and then a completely minimalistic, whispering, basic chorus. At first, I just didn't like being all belt-y right away.'

There was more tweaking to be done. Scooter Braun was very keen to add some hip-hop to the mix. 'Scooter was obsessed with bringing in the Ying Yang Twins,' said Wendy Goldstein. 'We had them try, but they just flopped it. They couldn't get it together.' Ariana then encouraged the team to grab Iggy Azalea for the recording. 'We figured it had to be a girl,' Kotecha told *Rolling Stone*. 'And there's so few big-name-female rappers in hip-hop. She came in without any drama, got behind the mic and just killed it.'

Then Max Martin came in and delivered his genius final touch. 'He came up with the horns and all those melodic things in the pre-chorus,' says Kotecha. 'Part of his genius is knowing that little thing that takes a song from eighty per cent to 100 per cent.' Kotecha was impressed with Ariana, too. Speaking of the song, he said: 'She's probably one of, if not the best, technical singers of her generation.'

The label bosses were popping metaphorical champagne corks. Charlie Walk, the executive vice president of Republic Records, said he just knew the song would be a hit the first time he heard it. 'It's the thirty second rule,' he explained to *Rolling Stone.* 'You know the difference between good and great in thirty seconds ... And in pop music now, there's a desperate need for proper vocalists that can sing a song the same way live it sounds on record. Kids can smell bullshit.'

The press, too, smelt a hit. MTV said the composition 'is so excitingly new but also decidedly so retro ... The cranky sax, the whispered chorus, the airy harmonies and Iggy's snarky feature all tied in with a juicy modern beat.'

Praise indeed wherever you look – yet 'Problem' almost never appeared on *My Everything* because of Ariana's initially negative feelings about the track. 'I didn't even want "Problem" on the album,' she told *Billboard* magazine. 'I fell out of love with it. Then we had a meeting with my label and Scooter [Braun] and my management, and we were all listening to music, and when "Problem" came on, I was like, "What the hell is wrong with me? Holy shit!"'

As a single, it was a smash. It proved to be the then fourth-largest debut week for a woman, and the biggest-ever debut for someone under twenty-one. 'Problem' also topped the iTunes chart in more than fifty countries. 'What it's done so far is just incredible in this day and age,' Tom Poleman, the president of National Programming Platforms for Clear Channel told *Rolling Stone.* It has become Ariana's signature tune – if you ask most pop fans to name an Ariana Grande song, they will not only say 'Problem', but probably launch into an impromptu rendition of the 'one less problem without ya …' refrain.

On dance-pop/EDM number 'One Last Time', Ariana further showcases her increased maturity and the scale of her intentions. The way that the despondency of the verses is offset by the more jolly, upbeat chorus, with its pounding drums and gorgeously simple synth, makes for a great listening experience. It was written and composed by Savan Kotecha, Rami Yacoub and Carl Falk, alongside producer Giorgio Tuinfort and French DJ David Guetta. Guetta had originally conceived the track for his own album, *Listen*, but while making the album, he told Idolator, he chose to give 'One Last Time' to Grande, since he 'had like 120 songs and [was] trying to make an album that ma[de] sense because some of the songs can be great, but that doesn't mean that they would fit together'.

It definitely worked: AXS's Lucas Villa praised Ariana's vocals on the song for 'exud[ing] sincerity and grace'. On Digital Spy, Lewis Corner named it a 'restrained sibling' of 'Break Free', having 'speckles of electronica to save it from falling into dwindling balladry'.

Co-written and co-produced by Ryan Tedder, on the track 'Why Try', Ariana really lets her diva out to play. Singing as if her very life is at stake, she is on great form on this power ballad. 'I love working with him because he understands what it's like as a vocalist to want the song that day,' said Ariana of Tedder in *Rolling Stone* 'He'll literally let me take two takes of something and then he'll have it done by the time I get out of the booth.'

On 'Break Free', Russian–German producer Zedd provides some kooky electronica and helps Ariana fulfil the title. It is a mesmerizing dance track with magnificent bass. 'Break Free' recalled Britney Spears in her 'Stronger' era, and Katy Perry in her 'Firework' prime.

Ariana herself described her song as 'fantastic and super-experimental for me'. She added: 'I never thought I'd do an EDM song, but that was an eye-opening experience, and now all I want to do is dance.' Though she would later confess to *Time* magazine that she had some issues with uber-producer Max Martin over some of the tracks grammatically incorrect lyrics. 'I fought him on it the whole time,' she said. 'I am not going to sing a grammatically incorrect lyric, help me, God! Max was like, "It's funny – just do it!" I know it's funny and silly, but grammatically incorrect things make me cringe sometimes.'

One such error in the lyrics is the talk of dying alive. Which seems bizarre, but as Ariana explained on MTV, it 'means life is so short – there's no reason to not enjoy it and there's no reason you should be anything but yourself. Have fun, be spontaneous and let go. It's OK to cut off whatever you feel is holding you back.' So, in the end, she let go of her issue with the wacky lyrics. 'I was like, whatever, let's do it and have some fun. I need to shake it off and let it go and be a little less rigid and old. I'm like ninety. I need to not be that old.'

Zedd explained how he wanted to collaborate with Ariana after hearing her voice for the first time during a showcase at Universal. He said, 'I was backstage and I heard someone sing. And I didn't know who it was, and I just said "I want to make a song with whoever is singing right now". I didn't know who it was, and it turned out being her. And luckily, now there's a song!'

On 'Break Free', co-producer Max Martin encouraged Ariana to sing in what she calls a 'more forward placement'. As she told *Billboard*: 'I was like no, no, no! Please just let me sing it how I would sing it,' she mock-whines. 'But he was like, "Just try it. Trust me".' In the end she was glad she did. 'I was so pleased when I tried something that I thought – no, that I knew I would hate.'

Big Sean is back for 'Best Mistake', the atmospheric, sultry ballad that got lots of minds wandering and tongues wagging over the extent of his relationship with Ariana. With its strings and emotive production, this is a true grower and was a clear pitch for the attention of the dance-floors of the planet.

Track seven is entitled 'Be My Baby'. It features another guest star – Norwegian DJ and musician Cashmere Cat. Although some critics felt that the predominance of guests in the middle of the album rather detracted from Ariana, here the guest certainly enhances it. This solid song is one that again lends weight to the argument that Ariana is the next Mariah Carey. *Billboard* dismissed this effort as 'far from Ariana's shining moment' on the album, but her throaty vocals are impressive.

She is back in defiant, scorned lover mode on 'Break Your Heart Right Back'. Here, the guest, actor and rapper Childish Gambino, is also an undoubted enhancer, rather than chancer in the overall experience. As one reviewer put it: he thumps his chest well. Ultimately, this track proves to be a call-to-arms for a generation of females, which is quite an achievement and very much in line with Ariana's hopes for the album overall.

However, then things take a turn for the less expected. On 'Love Me Harder', Ariana comes out with her most x-rated lyrics to date. Many eyebrows were raised by some of the topics covered in this song – some of those eyebrows belonging to the parents of young girls who overheard their daughters' listening habits. This song continues to be a controversial and widely discussed moment in Ariana's career. As such, it has produced a definite yardstick moment. Again, this is 'just what the Grande ordered'.

Her choice of guest star for 'Love Me Harder' was also unpredictable. As *Billboard* put it: 'Grande started on Nickelodeon, [Canadian singer songwriter] Abel Tesfaye started by singing "Codeine cups paint a picture so vivid" on his first mixtape.' And yet the collaboration works. With some retro guitar and Tesfaye's (aka the

Weeknd's) crooning vocals, one can almost forget how hardcore some of the lyrics are. Some critics felt that the presence of the 'sleazy' Weeknd alone took this song beyond the pale but for many listeners it was simply great fun.

Great anticipation focused on 'Just a Little Bit of Your Heart' because it was co-written with One Direction pin-up Harry Styles. The pop world had been on tenterhooks, waiting to hear what Styles' songwriting would sound like: would it sound as beautiful as he looked? Although the track itself was widely panned, there is no doubt that Ariana brings magic to it. For some listeners, the fact that she could lift such a moribund song showed her talent even more than her vocals on more winning material.

The high notes she hits in the chorus show her reach but ultimately the lyrics are too defeatist, particularly when compared to some of the album's more girlpower moments, for this track to be entirely palatable for many listeners. However, for Ariana it was important that her collection dealt with a true range of human emotions. She knew that life has its ups and downs and that, just as it is futile to pretend in day-to-day life that everything is great, so it was a mistake to broadcast a similar level of denial in your art.

Ariana reaches Rihanna-type territory with the track 'Hands on Me', another of *My Everything*'s more adult songs. Anyone who felt she remained tied to her Nickleodeon days will have been put right by this banger. Rapper A$AP Ferg proves an adequate guest but one who is almost forgotten amid Ariana's mature, sassy performance.

The title track closes the album, bringing the collection full circle, taking us back to the 'Intro' that kicked matters off. Starting off like an *X Factor* winner's single – one can imagine Leona Lewis doing the song justice – it sees Ariana in sensational vocal form. Perhaps the only complaint can be the track's brevity: at just two minutes and forty-eight seconds long, it leaves the listener hungry for more. Indeed, it is the lack of a massive, climactic final chorus that separates 'My Everything' from the reality show banger. All the same, the lyrics, which have the singer struggling to regain the firm footing she once had with her partner, are vulnerable and moving.

The album was widely praised by critics and fans, but before we turn to its fulsome praise, it is worth noting that not everyone was so positive. *The Guardian*, for instance, was less than blown away. Caroline Sullivan described it as 'faceless, generic bangerdom'. She added that it is 'difficult to engage with much of the synthy froth here'. Sadly, *The Guardian*'s sister paper, *The Observer*, was harsher still. Awarding the album just two of five stars, Kitty Empire wrote that on the album, 'every so often, a little shard of personality pierces the sheen'. She also complains that 'song after song goes by far too slickly… at the expense of lasting memories'.

Entertainment Weekly struck a similarly unimpressed chord. Critic Adam Markovitz said that Ariana had 'picked a set of songs so lyrically bland, sonically inoffensive, and artistically empty that they produce a zero-impact experience – musical vanilla fro-yo poured directly into your ears'. He concluded: 'She's got the voice. Now she just needs something to say with it.' At least this held out hope for the future.

Slant magazine, too, was critical. Andrew Chan wrote that 'the new album tries to expand her horizons with headache-inducing electro-pop and darker, edgier shades of R&B. In both lanes she sounds perfunctory and anonymous.' Although he felt that her voice 'can open the heavens', he was only willing to give *My Everything* two and a half stars out of five.

Thank goodness, then, for the many writers who heaped praise on the album. In *Billboard*, Jason Lipshutz was far more positive. He wrote that 'Problem' and 'Break Free' 'remain dizzying dance tunes', while 'One Last Time' and 'Why Try', 'possess the types of flawless melodies that are typically reserved for the world's biggest pop divas'. He concluded that Ariana had 'proven that her fizzy pop-R&B sound can get our hearts soaring' and hoped that in the future she could 'break them'.

Rolling Stone, too, was glowing in its verdict. Where other reviewers compared *My Everything* less than favourably with her debut album, Rob Sheffield took the opposite approach, saying that the follow-up 'is where the twenty-one-year-old Nickelodeon starlet grows up. It's a confident, intelligent, brazen pop statement, mixing bubblegum diva vocals with EDM break beats.' Pleasingly for Ariana, he added that 'when she reaches for a more adult tone ... she pulls it off', before concluding: 'It sounds like there's no limit to where Ariana Grande can go from here. But as *My Everything* proves, she's already a major force.'

Meanwhile in *Pitchfork*, critic Meaghan Garvey wrote that in the work Ariana 'ditches the manic-Disney-dream-girl ballads and goes straight for the bangers; while it may not be as consistent a statement as *Yours Truly*, it's refreshingly grown-up'. Garvey concluded that *My Everything* 'feels like Grande's arrival as a true pop fixture, not just a charming novelty ... Grande slowly but confidently comes into her own; and while her personality may still take a backseat to her technical skill, it's beginning to wink through the theatrics. Turns out, so-called mini-Mariah can hold her own in 2014; and while the best songs here may not be timeless, they certainly feel right for right now.'

The *Los Angeles Times* heaped praise on Ariana's 'newfound swagger' and 'empowering ascent'. Mikael Wood said that 'what leaves an impression is Grande herself, deeply cheerful yet with guns blazing, an innocent newcomer no more'. AllMusic chipped in with a briefer notice, which argued that 'she functions as a likeable pop ringleader, stepping aside when the track calls for it and then unleashing a full-throated wail when it's her time to shine'. Stephen Thomas Erlewine also enjoyed the 'serious EDM flourishes and a facility with hip-hop'.

Even AV's Annie Zaleski, who gave *My Everything* a disappointing C+ verdict, said that the 'slick throwback … further establishes Grande as a consummate performer and vocal interpreter'. Final word to *USA Today*'s Elysa Gardner, who wrote that the album has 'ample evidence of Grande's girlish playfulness – and a sense of growing confidence, from the pumping strong-woman number "Break Free" to "Hands on Me", which is in the taut, teasing vein of "Problem" but with more textural and rhythmic sophistication'. She added that 'Blending sugar and spice, *My Everything* reaches out to everyone in Grande's growing fan base.'

The *New York Daily News* complained that 'the constant jerking back and forth between styles interrupts any sense of flow. As musical journeys go, this one mimics a packed crosstown bus, stopping and starting in jammed traffic.' The *Huffington Post* said that the sophomore album from the former Nickelodeon star cements her in that category of, 'Uh, Hey, This Woman Has An Incredible Voice', naming *My Everything* one of its twenty-three best albums of 2014.

It was to a backdrop of these verdicts that *My*

Everything was released to the public on 25 August 2014 by Republic Records – less than twelve months after her debut emerged. Ariana was thrilled to have a successor on the shelves. She felt this took her from the stature of a pop star with one release under her belt to more accomplished and sustained territory. In short, it made her feel all grown up.

In the build-up to the official launch she had been her usual canny operator self online. In the weeks preceding the album's release she released previews of the songs to the public, to pique their interest and excitement. On 7 July, Ariana posted on Instagram a teaser of 'Best Mistake'. Then came teasers of other tracks including 'Be My Baby' and 'Love Me Harder', before MTV released 'Why Try', 'Be My Baby', 'Love Me Harder' and 'Just a Little Bit of Your Heart'.

On the eve of the album's release, she opened the 2014 MTV Video Music Awards with a glorious live rendition of 'Break Free'. She returned to the stage later to run through 'Bang Bang' with Jessie J and Nicki Minaj. The public relations blitz continued in the immediate aftermath of the album's drop. On 29 August, Ariana performed 'Problem', 'Break Free', 'Bang Bang', and 'Break Your Heart Right Back' on the huge US TV series *Today*. With a group of devoted fans around the famous plaza, Ariana was on great form. Her appearance on *Today* was more than a mere musical one, however. As *Today* reported, she 'ended up taking over the better part of the broadcast, too'. She gave a weather forecast as well as inviting her grandmother on set for an interview of her own. Classic Ariana: full of mischief, confidence and humour. She may have been cheeky but the crew could not help but love her.

On and on rolled the Ariana public relations train. The following week, Ariana performed the title track from *My Everything* during the *Stand Up to Cancer* telethon. She dedicated her performance to her grandfather, who had died from cancer earlier that year. Even in the midst of a night of such emotion, and surrounded by such luminaries as Jennifer Aniston, Halle Berry, Reese Witherspoon, Kiefer Sutherland, Will Ferrell and Ben Stiller, Ariana stood out for the sheer emotional sincerity of her rendition and the charisma with which she rendered the track.

It had been a triumphant and memorable publicity campaign for the new album. Now, Ariana and her team could sit back and see how well it sold. According to *Billboard*, *My Everything* shifted over 160,000 copies in its first week from the shelves of physical outlets and Internet stores. It debuted at number one on the *Billboard* 200. In 2016, the Recording Industry Association of America (RIAA) certified the album double platinum and, in Japan, it remained at the summit of the iTunes Store chart for nine weeks, thus earning Grande the longest at number one in 2014, breaking the previous record held by *Frozen: Original*

Motion Picture Soundtrack. At the fifty-seventh Annual Grammy Awards in 2015, *My Everything* was nominated for Best Pop Vocal Album.

However, while critical and commercial success have always been important to Ariana to an extent, the real critic she wanted to impress was, in many ways, herself. How would she feel about *My Everything*, when all was done and dusted? 'I'm a perfectionist, so I never thought I'd be able to say this, but I love this album five times as much as *Yours Truly*,' she told *Billboard*. 'They're different, but I love this one so much more.'

One Friday night in September, controversial singer Chris Brown shared his fantasy-themed video for the track 'Don't Be Gone Too Long', featuring Ariana. Coming from his forthcoming album *X*, the track excited Arianators. Ultimately, though, it did not happen. After Brown received a prison sentence in connection with a fight in Washington, the single was scrapped. When the album version of the track appeared, her vocals had been replaced by Cathy Dennis (the song's writer).

Ariana had dodged a bullet there by avoiding becoming embroiled in the contentious world of Chris Brown. A more successful hook-up came in the form of 'All My Love': a song by American electronic music project Major Lazer. The track, featuring Ariana's vocals, appeared on the *The Hunger Games: Mockingjay, Part 1* soundtrack. Ariana announced on Twitter that it was 'a very interesting song. It's very different.'

She had two albums on the shelves and a whole new level of recognition – but if anyone thought Ariana was about to start taking it easy, they were wrong. Her success only made her hungry for more. Whenever she reached a new height, she was too busy looking for the next one to stay still. In particular, she wanted to get back into the studio. For Ariana, studio work is not a sideshow in her career – it is at the heart of it. As she told *Billboard*: 'I have to launch this album, and I get to do a tour, which all sounds fine and dandy ... but I just love being in the studio. I could start a new album right now, tonight. That sounds the most enticing to me. I love it.'

The year of her second album's release was also notable for Ariana's performance at the White House, where she performed a live mini-show for Barack and Michelle Obama and their guests in March, as part of the 'Women of Soul' concert arranged by the US First Lady. Other performers included Aretha Franklin, Patti LaBelle, Melissa Etheridge, Janelle Monáe, Tessanne Chin and Jill Scott. Ariana sang Whitney Houston's 'I Have Nothing' and her own track 'Tattooed Heart'.

The following month she was back at the White House, to sing at the annual Easter Egg Roll. Wearing just an oversized purple sweater and white go-go boots, Ariana sang 'Right There' for the 30,000-strong audience with confidence and aplomb. For her, there was no doubt about the highlight of the day. She later wrote on Twitter: 'Met my childhood crush Jim Carrey … he was kind, warm and human. I'm so happy.'

To have sung at the White House once would have been honour enough for many artists. To have sung twice at the White House during an entire career would be considered a breathtaking achievement. To have sung twice in a *year* – twice in two months, in fact – was mindbending for her. On a good day, and these days were good indeed, she felt like everything was going well. She was on track in her career and rolling along nicely.

However, she also knew that she could not control everything about how her career developed. With her rising stock as a musical artist, came increased fame. With increased fame, came greater vulnerability to scandal. As she was about to discover, the media might build you up – but it can also take great delight in knocking you down …

Above left: Performing at the MTV EMAs in Glasgow, Scotland, 2014.

Above right: Ariana on stage at the KIIS FM Jingle Ball in Los Angeles, 2014.

Below: Ariana at the Disney Parks Unforgettable Christmas Celebration in Florida, 2015.

Above left: Performing at the American Music Awards, Los Angeles, 2015, where she won the award for Best Pop/Rock Female Artist.

Above right: Ariana posing with Minnie Mouse at the Disney Parks Unforgettable Christmas Celebration, 2015.

Left: Ariana arriving at the airport in Tokyo to the delight of her many fans, 2016.

Above: On the promotional tour again, this time performing in Paris, 2016.

Below: At the Capital FM Summertime Ball in London, 2016.

Above: Posing for a photo with Rita Ora at the MTV Video Music Awards in New York, 2016.

Below: Accepting her award for Artist of the Year at the 2016 American Music Awards in Los Angeles.

Right: Performing in Miami on her *Dangerous Woman* tour, April 2017.

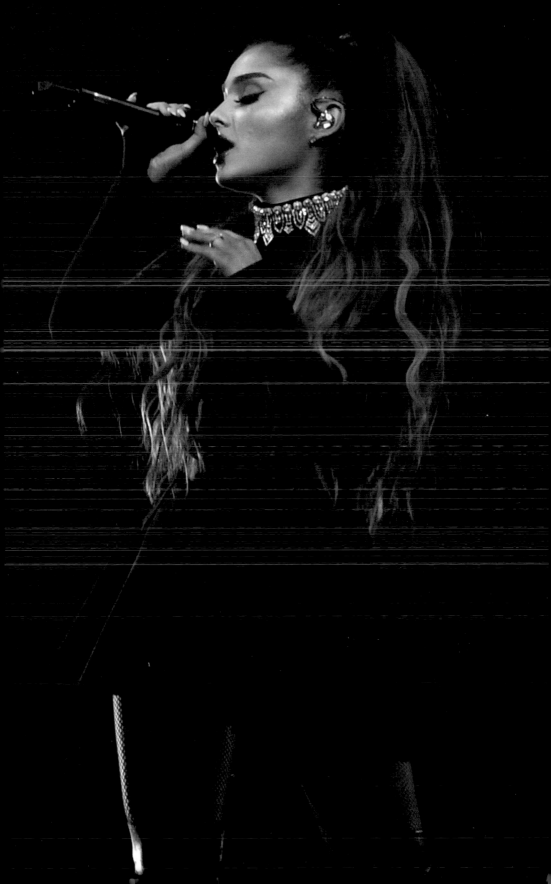

Ariana performing at the One Love Manchester benefit concert in June 2017, which she organized to raise money for the victims of the deadly terrorist attack at her show a few weeks earlier.

CHAPTER SEVEN

STORMY SEAS

During 2014, Ariana was schooled on the realities of fame and how your image can be tossed back and forth like a ship on wild waters. To continue the nautical metaphor, she first faced a tidal wave of negative insinuations, a wave that threatened to turn into a tsunami. Then, by wresting control of her destiny, she steered it to happier waters, where a more accurate image could be reflected. All in all, then, it would prove a stormy journey. One that started with a lot of trouble for our heroine. Up until then, she had received mostly positive press for the early stages of her career. True, there were sometimes reports or reviews she could have done without in an ideal world. But much of her coverage was nice. However, during 2014, she suddenly noticed that negative and unpleasant stories were starting to fly about. She felt that many of them were distorted – or just plain untrue. As she read some of the racy headlines and sensationalist stories about her, Ariana simply did not recognize the young lady being portrayed. She was appalled that people could make these accusations.

All of this was a harsh lesson for her. She learned quickly, but bitterly, that just as the media can be your best friend, writing great things about you and your work and helping to promote sales of your music, it could also be your worst enemy. She also spotted a 'bandwagon' effect to the media mob: once one journalist or outlet wrote something critical of you, others would seem to scramble to find their own mud to sling. Whatever the latest trend was, the media would follow it. For Ariana, just twenty as the year dawned, this was a tough lesson.

In her case, the mud thrown at her increasingly took the form of suggestions that she was a 'difficult' star, one who made unreasonable demands of those around her; one who was unpleasant and disingenuous with her fans; one who made life hell for journalists and photographers, and hissed around backstage at charity events. Who was this lady, wondered Ariana as she read the sensationalist stories?

When she had previously been occasionally accused of diva-like behaviour, she had mostly kept quiet, preferring not to dignify the allegations with any sort of official response. However, in 2014, as the allegations mounted by the day, she did speak up. Horrified by what she was facing in the media, she described the suggestion that she is a diva as 'totally untrue and annoying'.

Speaking to Mike E and Emma on Australia's radio 96.1, Ariana said that when she faces the diva allegation, she prefers to say to herself: 'You know what? That's unreal. It's nonsense. My fans know who I am, my family knows who I am, my friends know who I am – and that's all that matters.' Having clearly given the matter a lot of thought, she also said that this was part of a wider issue, which all people face. 'No matter what you do, no matter what your profession is, no matter how old you are, everybody deals with haters,' she argued. Finally, she said, many of those who criticize her 'don't know me or understand me'. To her, that was what mattered most.

However, it was hard for her to shake off the production line of accusations that were flung about her during 2014. A particularly damaging allegation came from one of her own fans, Jennifer O'Connor, who hit the headlines after she left a negative description on the photo-sharing website Instagram, of a meeting with Ariana. 'I'm just gonna say this,' began O'Connor, perhaps not realizing at this stage what a storm she was about to stir up. 'Fame gets to a lot of people's heads, & it got to Ariana Grande's. She was nice in the beginning rushing through the first 15 seconds of the

30 second "hanging out" session that I won along with two other people. But when she saw my sister taking pics of me handing her my drawings, that I worked so hard on, Ariana made her delete them and then she just left.' As for Jennifer's sister, Kelly, she addressed Ariana directly, saying: 'My sister & I were huge fans. u made @ HerNamesJen extremely sad by walking away from her & telling me to delete all my pics.'

Recalling a happier encounter with Ariana in 2011, she added that the star of 2014 was 'Not the Ariana I remember meeting 3½ years ago. I'm just sharing my experience so that's it. No I don't "hate" her or anything. I'm just really disappointed at how fast people can lose themselves.'

This was about to become a major showbiz story, another example of a comment on social media becoming a big deal in the mainstream media, as the lines between the two increasingly blurred.

The story only expanded further when O'Connor's father subsequently gave a lengthier description of the two encounters the girls had written about. Remembering the first meeting, in January 2011, he wrote that, after Ariana tweeted that she was 'visiting the Titanic exhibit at the Las Vegas Luxor hotel', his daughter had asked if they could go along to see if they could see 'her idol'. They waited on a bench near the exit of the exhibition 'for hours' before Ariana eventually appeared. He said Ariana noticed Jen smiling at her, and asked if she would like a photo with her. After chatting for a few minutes with Jen, Ariana posed for a photo. 'It was a wonderful experience and Jen has told the world about it for years,' he continued. Ariana was 'one of the nicest celebrities we have ever encountered', he said, adding that 'we have come across a lot of them'.

However, he too had complaints about the subsequent meeting in 2014 – and he was willing to go to town on the matter. Jen won a contest thrown by MTV to meet Ariana in Los Angeles. Taking her older sister along as her permitted 'plus one', she arrived early at the venue and Ariana arrived late, whereupon she 'approached her fans without a smile – just an icy look as she toyed with her hair', he claims. He says Jen was then given a series of rules about what she would and would not be allowed to do, including that they could take a selfie with Ariana, but no other photos. Then Ariana 'spent perhaps 15 seconds with each of them', he alleges.

The trouble really started when Kelly took a photo of Jen showing Ariana one of her drawings. It is alleged that Ariana snapped: 'Delete those pictures, please,' and then, when Kelly asked whether she could keep just one, Ariana responded by turning to her staff and saying: 'Make sure she deleted those.' She then reportedly left without saying goodbye.

Jennifer and Kelly's father concluded by saying that he did not expect miracles from the encounter, but, given that it was a competition prize, rather than an unplanned street encounter, '15 seconds each, followed by barked orders to delete photos, and an abrupt exit' did not seem fair or kind.

Ariana watched these allegations cause a stir and decided that in this case it would be wise to respond. Her explanation was that she was still grieving after the death of her grandfather. 'A fan gave me a photo of me & my grandpa. I walked away because I didn't want them to see me start to cry,' she wrote on Twitter. Ariana continued: 'I am still in mourning and I wrote a letter to have sent to her afterward but MTV told me they had already left. My heart is still healing and it's moments like that that make it real again that he's gone ...'

However, these words were not enough to placate everyone. Several commentators disputed elements of Ariana's explanation. For instance, the flashpoint in the O'Connor account came as Ariana was handed a drawing of herself, not a family photograph. Also, as some writers pointed out, the explanatory letter that Ariana mentioned could still have been sent to Jen after the day in question, thus perhaps helping to smooth over the dispute.

Although this was a memorable fuss, it was far from the only one. A separate flashpoint came when Ariana did the media rounds in Australia. Again, deleted photographs were at the heart of the drama. Ahead of the promotional interviews, various rules were handed to media outlets.

These guidelines affected both the journalists who would interview her, and the photographers booked in to snap her. Among the subject matters considered off limits for interviewers were her romantic relationships, Mariah Carey, collaboration with Justin Bieber, her late grandfather and her Nickelodeon series *Sam & Cat*.

Photographers, too, were given directives: don't use natural light, and don't shoot from the right-hand side of her face. During a photoshoot for Australian newspaper *mX*, Ariana checked each shot after it was taken and asked for images she didn't like to be deleted. According to news.com.au, after a few minutes she 'left the hotel suite, complaining to her reps that she was unhappy with how her top looked in the poses'. After twenty minutes of waiting for Ariana to return, one of her team appeared, allegedly ordering the *mX* photographer to delete all his photos. When the photographer refused, tension rose. He was later approached by one of Ariana's bodyguards, who tried to stop the photographer closing his car boot, after he had put his photography equipment in there. Needless, perhaps, to say, Ariana did not return for any of the day's other scheduled photo sessions.

It is important to recognize at this point how much of this is commonplace. In show business, the 'talent' often makes requests ahead of an interview or a photoshoot. They might ask for upsetting topics to be avoided during questioning, or even topics that they feel they have already been asked about a million times. As for tetchiness over photographs, in an industry so fundamentally based on image and appearance, it is perhaps not unreasonable for stars to feel a little uptight about photographs.

The reader could consider whether they have ever taken a photo of themselves for Facebook or Instagram, and then decided to delete it and try taking a new one from a different angle. Many young people will have done this, and their photo will normally only be seen by a couple of hundred people at most. For Ariana, photographs of her will be seen by millions across the world. So, is she being a diva, or is she actually in many ways the same as any of us, just in a different context?

Having met Ariana, *E!* television anchor Giuliana Rancic would argue the former. The broadcaster reported: 'I think she does have a little bit of a diva thing going on', after Ariana made Rancic film her from her favourite side during a red carpet interview. 'She came up on the platform, and normally I stand on this side [her left side] to the camera,' remembered Rancic.

'Little Ariana comes over, I feel like "bing", elbow in my side, I'm like, "What's going on?" and they push me to the other side. So I had to be on my ugly side.' For Rancic, part of the issue was Ariana's age and what she perceived as her level of experience and stature. 'I just felt like it's one thing if it's Mariah, you know, I'll get on any side, I'll bend down, I'll climb a ladder, whatever it takes to get Mariah to do an interview.'

There seems to be an element of ageism to this particular attack on Ariana. If such demands are unacceptable from a young star, it seems flawed to suggest that one would deal with them happily should a more veteran talent echo them. However, Rancic had helped open up the floodgates – and then came an avalanche of allegations. It was as if the media has sniffed blood and wanted to go in for the kill. For Ariana, her loved ones and her fans, it was hard to watch a young woman increasingly mauled by the media pack.

The *New York Post*'s infamously brutal Page Six column claimed that Ariana's life coach had quit working with her because he could no longer tolerate her ways. The report claimed that the singer, 'plagued by rumours of a bad attitude', had become so difficult that her life coach had 'walked off the job months ago because he just couldn't handle her attitude'. 'He just couldn't take it anymore,' said the alleged source. 'Everything people are saying about her is true.' In a previous report, the same section had spread allegations about Ariana, saying: 'She kind of speaks down to everyone around her', claiming that this made for a 'very intense' atmosphere. In a yet further dig at her, the source said that when Grande arrives at an event 'It's like the president is in town'.

All of this began to paint a picture of Ariana that was far from agreeable to her. However, there was worse to come, because perhaps the most potentially damaging allegation came in the *New York Daily News*. The claims centred on a promotional visit Ariana paid to a Manhattan radio station during the summer of 2014. According to an 'industry insider', Ariana was gracious with fans when she arrived, but then immediately changed her attitude once they were out of sight. 'She did autographs and pics and was all smiles until she got into the elevator,' said the source. 'And as soon as the doors shut she said, "I hope they all f—king die".' This was a devastating allegation. The report turned into more than just an attack on Ariana. It said the alleged bad behaviour was no surprise, because she is managed by the 'smarmy' Scooter Braun.

It added that she 'further dissed fans' by stipulating that the $495 photo op for fans during her Honeymoon Tour would be only for group photos of four to six people, not individual shots. 'Really?' responded one industry commentator. 'Bieber, Miley, Britney, Katy Perry all did individual pics when they sold these packages.'

Ariana disputed these allegations and looked around for people to support her. Surely, she felt, she would not be expected to face such a storm alone? Help would come – but only after more trouble. In the same month, someone stood up to defend her as she faced another allegation. An unnamed 'insider' told the *Daily Star* that Ariana 'was a total nightmare' at the Los Angeles fundraiser Stand Up to Cancer. 'At first, it was her warning the lighting crew if they used red spotlights she would go berserk,' claimed the insider. 'But then she kept everyone waiting while other stars came in and did their thing.' The shadowy source said that Ariana was ruder than Lady Gaga, Madonna and Mariah 'combined'.

However, the 'insider' remained unnamed – and many celebrities suspect that stories based on such mysterious sources are exaggerated or entirely made up. In any case, the Stand Up To Cancer boss Joel Gallen said himself that the story was 'completely false'. Finally, Ariana had a knight in shining armour to protect her. Speaking to *E! News*, Gallen said: 'Ariana was wonderful to work with, very gracious and a consummate professional to our team and everyone at the Stand Up to Cancer telecast.' For Ariana's fans, this was the end of the matter. After all, Gallen had witnessed Ariana at first hand, and that is always more convincing than unnamed tittle-tattle.

The British pop star Jessie J certainly subscribes to that way of thinking. The former judge on the reality show *The Voice* went into bat to help Ariana. In doing so, she got to the heart of the issue. 'I always say, judge a person when you meet them,' she told *US Weekly*. 'I've met Ariana, and there's a very thin line between "diva" and "survival". And a lot of people can't [differentiate that] – and I've had that.'

As she said, Jessie, too, had been accused of having

just the same sort of character. 'I've had the diva stuff,' she said. 'And it's when people can't cope with how passionate you are and how much you care. She's super talented, she's very young, and she's very sure of what she wants. I think she's wonderful. She's great.' Could, therefore, the ferocity of the accusations Ariana faced be a measure and reflection of the passion she held for her career?

As for Ariana herself, she repeatedly denies behaving badly. She also tries to not take the fuss too seriously, after realizing that if you are thrown about at the whims of the media then you are truly powerless. Instead, she tried to respond with dignity and a splash of wit to the entire saga. Asked if she were a diva, she said: 'Celine Dion is a diva, thank you. But if you want to call me a bitch, that's not accurate. Because it's just not in my nature.'

In response to the suggestion she left the Australian photoshoot early, she said she only left to change her outfit and the photographer said 'ridiculous, untrue things' about her. More generally, she told *Entertainment Tonight*, it was the dishonesty of the claims that made her most angry. 'If any of the things they were saying were true I wouldn't mind it,' she said.

It had been a tough time for her, and it ended with a new allegation: that she demanded to be carried when she was tired. 'Her new rule is that she has to be carried – literally carried like a baby – when she doesn't feel like walking,' said a source in *Life & Style* magazine. 'Ariana is such a diva.'

However, in this instance, Big Sean was able to respond personally. During an interview with *The Breakfast Club*, he said: 'That don't even sound logical. No, man, she don't get carried. I remember I was with her one time and she got carried but it was 'cause her foot was bleeding. She busted her foot, you know, dancing and stuff. That's ridiculous.' It was another incidence of how an innocent moment can be twisted into a drama by anyone if they are desperate for an angle.

What a storm in a teacup these issues proved to be. Ariana feels, and hopes, that the 'diva' allegation will disappear in time. 'It's funny how a certain amount of success comes with a certain amount of weird, inaccurate depictions of you,' she said in the *Daily Telegraph*. 'But I feel like it will die down because it's not something that I pay into. And also things can only last so long when there's little truth to them. So that's why I don't trip over it.'

Republic Records chair Monte Lipman also spoke up for Ariana. 'The D-word for Ariana is "do-it-yourself",' said Lipman in *Billboard*. 'She takes on tremendous responsibility and isn't afraid to challenge whomever. Some people are intimidated by that, but I encourage it … We've argued – we'll raise our voices – but that's creative conflict and that's where the sparks fly. It always starts and ends with Ariana.'

Final word on the diva allegations saga should go to

Ariana's manager, Scooter Braun. Taking to Twitter, he wrote that his treasured client is 'kind, caring, and more than anything she is a great human being'. Turning his attention to those who portray her as a diva, he added: 'Some people make up [rumours] for a living ... so ...' It was a suitably sassy comment on the saga by a man who had himself got caught up in it personally.

Ariana and her team knew that they could issue all the refuting comments they liked but ultimately the best way to get a nagging news narrative to go away is to create a better one: distraction is always better than denial. Given the burning feelings that Ariana had on a particular issue, it seemed just the right moment for her to speak up. In doing so, she would drown out the critics and instead spark a chorus of praise for herself, as she took the lead on this one.

Helpfully, the matter she wanted to speak out on was somewhat connected to the narrative she wanted to bury. She was beginning to wonder, given this litany of criticism she had faced for her alleged behaviour, if there were double standards at play. Although male pop stars such as Justin Bieber have sometimes been accused of diva-like behaviour, it seemed that such allegations were reserved particularly for female music artists.

Ariana had had enough of this – and decided to speak out about how she felt. She began by showing a journalist from *Billboard* a collection of tweets from a British radio station, which she felt illustrated a problem.

Two of the tweets heaped praise on Justin Bieber and Zayn Malik for posing with little or no clothing, and two criticize Miley Cyrus and Kim Kardashian for doing the same thing. The double standards were not limited to this radio station – many pop culture analysts have pointed out that they are endemic across the mainstream media. By raising the issue, though, Ariana was showing principle and courage.

But her fight had only just begun. In the same *Billboard* interview, she also railed against the media's tendency to only describe female celebrities in terms of the men they have dated, rather than by their own achievements. 'I'll never be able to swallow the fact that people feel the need to attach a successful woman to a man when they say her name,' she said. 'I saw a headline – draw your own conclusions [on the subjects] because it'll be so much drama that I don't want – they called someone another someone's ex, and that pissed me off. This person has had so many great records in the last year, and she hasn't been dating him forever. Call her by her name!' Warming, or rather simmering, to her theme, she continued: 'I hate that. Like, I'm fuming. Sorry. You opened up ... I need to take a sip of water and breathe.'

A momentum had begun – and Ariana would continue speaking up on sexism. During an interview with *Billboard*, she said: 'If you're going to rave about how sexy a male artist looks with his shirt off, and a woman decides to get in her panties or show her boobies for a photoshoot, she needs to be treated with the same awe and admiration. I will say it until I'm an old-ass lady with my tits out at Whole Foods. I'll be in the produce aisle, naked at ninety-five, with a sensible ponytail, one strand of hair left on my head and a Chanel bow. Mark my words. See you there with my ninety-five dogs.'

Typical Ariana: she took a serious issue that made her burn with anger but delivered her manifesto on it with as much wit as anger. By painting with words that portrait of her as an older woman, she was showing that while she took the issue very seriously, she did not take herself that seriously at all. This was a smart move: all too often, when women speak up about sexism, some critics attempt to paint them as being in the throes of a humourless huff. But no one was going to be able to do this easily for Ariana. She had vented with vim.

However, these comments did not quench the burning sense of injustice inside her. She noticed that the media trends she despaired of continued to haunt her and other female celebrities. After she split from rapper Big Sean, she was linked in the media to Niall Horan of One Direction. Although she understood that interest in her private life came with the territory of fame, Ariana nevertheless wondered why she was increasingly referred to in the media not in relation to her music, but only in relation to men she had dated, was dating or might date in the future. Was there no end to this nonsense?

This was part of a wider trend in the media, which seemed to disproportionately affect female celebs. Even years after a famous woman had split from a male star, she would be referred to in terms of their break-up. For instance, if she were photographed going to get a latte from a coffee store, the accompanying headline would read that she was showing her famous ex that she would 'not be beaten'. Whereas in fact, she was just going to get a coffee.

This frustrated and enraged a lot of famous women, Ariana included. Finally, in June 2015, her patience snapped and she decided to really go to town on the issue. She posted a lengthy essay on social media, taking the world to task for this and other sexist trends. From the very first line she showed that she was in a bold, outspoken and sassy mood. 'being "empowered" … is not the same as being as being a "bitch",' she wrote.

Continuing what would become an important piece of writing, viewed by millions of people around the world, she added: 'I am tired of living in a world where women are mostly referred to as a man's past, present, or future PROPERTY / POSSESSION.' Ariana also explained that this issue had been on her mind for some time. 'I'm saying this after literally 8 years of feeling like I constantly had to have a boy by my side,' she wrote. 'After being on my own now for a few months I am realizing that that's just not the case … I have never felt more present, grounded, and satisfied.

I've never laughed harder or had more fun or enjoyed my life more.'

She spoke of the prospect of progress. Not for Ariana the despairing tone – rather, she preferred the call to arms. 'I can't wait to live in a world where people are not valued by who they're dating / married to / attached to / having sex with (or not) / seen with ... but by their value as an individual. I want the people reading this to know that they are MORE THAN enough on their own,' she continued.

The response to this was powerful – and praise for her words came from several corners and was immediate and fulsome. 'I'm so proud of you, always. But especially today,' Taylor Swift posted on Twitter.

'It's vitally important when celebrities and people with high public profiles speak openly and clearly about discrimination,' added feminist writer Soraya Chemaly on CNN. 'For a very long time, it seemed as though young women in the public eye were particularly cautious about revealing their experiences with sexism. But in the past two years, there has been a refreshing shift away from that and towards smart commentary on double standards that really affect people's lives.' Writing in *E! News*, Kendall Fisher described Ariana as a feminist hero.

Ariana's writing on the issue continued. 'ppl are so ignorant sometimes,' she tweeted. 'stop trying to make people feel badly about their bodies. it's okay to be different ... to be curvy or to be thin. when did it become socially acceptable to comment on what you think is "wrong" with other people's bodies?'

After an online snark criticized Ariana's appearance in a video alongside Nicki Minaj, Ariana explained on MTV: 'we were having fun! dancing on stage … how about we respect people's body boundaries and encourage each other to feel like a babe no matter how they are? that [would] be nice. so tired of watching everyone try to tear each other down.'

A similar issue arose when a male tweeter said he would prefer Ariel Winter to Ariana. Why? Because, he wrote, he prefers 'curvy' women to 'sticks' like Ariana. 'we live in a day and age where people make it IMPOSSIBLE for women, men, anyone to embrace themselves exactly how they are. diversity is sexy! loving yourself is sexy! you know what is NOT sexy? misogyny, objectifying, labeling, comparing and body shaming!!! talking about people's body's as if they're on display ASKING for your approval / opinion. THEY ARE NOT!!!!'

On and on have come her magnificent mini manifestoes on Twitter. 'when will people stop being offended by women showing skin / expressing sexuality? men take their shirts off / express their sexuality on stage, in videos, on instagram, anywhere they want to … all. the. time. the double standard is so boring and exhausting. with all due respect, i think it's time you get your head out of your ass. women can love their bodies too!!'

She took her position and shared it across different media platforms. For her, this was a long-term struggle – a lifetime one, perhaps. Not something she was just touching base on briefly. When she was asked during a radio interview for Los Angeles Power 106 what she would do if she had to choose between her mobile phone or her make-up, she gave the question short shrift. 'Is this what you think girls have trouble choosing between? Is this men assuming that that's what girls would have to choose between? You need a little brushing up on equality over here,' she said. 'I have a long list of things I'd like to change … I think, judgment in general. Intolerance, meanness, double standards, misogyny, racism, sexism … There's lots we've got to get started on.'

Her comments are not merely outbursts, or rants, though. In fact, she shows great diplomacy when necessary. For instance, when actress and singer-songwriter Bette Midler slammed Ariana for what she saw as an over-revealing photoshoot with *The Guardian.* Midler said: 'You don't have to make a whore out of yourself to get ahead.' Ariana took the Twitter high road and responded with a winning combination of fire and respect. 'Bette was always a feminist who stood for women being able to do whatever the F they wanted without judgement!' she said. 'Not sure where that Bette went but I want that sexy mermaid back!!! Always a fan no matter what my love.'

A happier media circus focused on Ariana's new fragrance, Frankie, which she launched in 2015. A non-gender-exclusive scent, she named it in honour of her older brother – whose name can be for a boy or girl. Fragrances have become a sideline for her: the following year she created another one titled Sweet Like Candy, then, on Solar Eclipse day in 2017, Ariana announced the arrival of her third, referred to as Moonlight by Ariana Grande. The accompanying press release stated, 'It was created to inspire confidence to be yourself and carries the strong message of being a positive light to those around you,' she said of the latter, again borrowing the Kabbalah's ever-present theme of bringing light to the world.

Thanks in large part to her spirituality, Ariana was learning to deal with the storms of her career well. She remained strong and reminded herself that what mattered most was what she was really like – not how people who did not know her regarded her. This strength and poise would serve her well during 2015, because a scandal was about to erupt that would dwarf any she had faced before.

#donutgate

If she thought 2014 had been stormy, then 2015 was going to offer a whole new level of drama – and if you want a snapshot of how crazy her life can be, then consider this fact: the almighty storm was whipped up by a humble doughnut. Not only that, but by the time the storm had subsided, Ariana would have lost a gig at the White House because of it.

Celebrity scandals are all part and parcel of the show-business industry. Particularly for the media, these are not an unfortunate by-product of the sector, but rather a central and crucial component of it all. There have always been scandals and dramas among famous folk, perhaps made worse by the rise of television in the 1950s and the growing power of the media. But in the twenty-first century, with the expansion and then explosion of social media, this has taken on a new intensity. On top of tabloid newspapers and celebrity gossip magazines, there are now television channels devoted purely to show-business chatter, and, of course, websites and giant social media accounts. This has caused the appetite for celebrity scandal to move from hungry to ravenous.

Whether it's leaked intimate photographs and videos, high-profile affairs and divorces, admissions into rehab for various addictions, or all-out meltdowns, the menu is varied. Well, if you thought that some of these scandals centred on bizarre themes, then the doughnut storm, inevitably nicknamed 'doughnut-gate' by the media, was about to reach a whole new level of weirdness.

It all started on 4 July as Ariana and her new love interest, backup dancer Ricky Alvarez, upset staff members at a doughnut shop in Lake Elsinore, California with their behaviour. At one point, CCTV footage shows the pair sharing a couple of kisses but when a fresh batch of doughnuts was placed on the counter, the singer is heard saying: 'What the f**k is that? I hate Americans. I hate America.' She then laughed out loud after Alvarez seemingly licked a doughnut and walked away.

When the footage was published on celebrity gossip website TMZ, it caused an immediate stir. Things got worse when twenty-two-year-old Mayra Solis, a cashier on duty at the doughnut shop on the day, alleged that not only did Ariana not purchase any of the doughnuts but also 'she was really rude'.

There was talk of Ariana facing criminal charges over the incident – until a representative for the Riverside County Sheriff's department announced that the owner of the Wolfee Donuts shop would not press charges. Then TMZ reported that the shop had failed a health inspection due to the incident. The business was told one of the reasons for it not passing the inspection was down to 'customers licking donuts incorrectly placed on counter'. It was given a week to resolve the issue and had its Health Department 'A' rating downgraded to a 'B' while the issue was resolved.

Joe Marin, owner of the shop, told the People website: 'We got a B because the donuts were on top of the tray, and we were actually stocking up. My employees kept going in the back and grabbing some more. They were minor things: little, tiny, minor things that were fixed in three days.' Health officials focused on why the doughnuts were left exposed and whether the shop had a history of the practice, as California health laws require restaurants to keep food protected from the public.

'During the investigation, the manager did state they normally don't leave donuts out like was shown in the video,' Dottie Ellis-Merki, a spokeswoman for the Riverside County Department of Environment, told the Associated Press. 'The employee went to the back to retrieve freshly made donuts by request of the customer and left the trays out while getting other trays.'

Ariana quickly felt besieged as the drama grew and grew. She knew from watching other scandals unfold that sometimes one seemingly simple incident can snowball into something much bigger. She cancelled her much-anticipated gig at baseball's All-Star Game, being replaced by Demi Lovato. Ariana also said on Buzzfeed that she was sorry for backing out of the MLB All-Star Concert. 'As for why I cannot be at the MLB show, I have had emergency oral surgery and due to recovery I cannot attend the show,' she said in a statement. 'I hope to make it up to all those fans soon.'

On YouTube, in her first fulsome response to the doughnut incident, she said: 'I am EXTREMELY proud to be an American, and I've always made it clear that I love my country.' Ariana added: 'What I said in a private moment with my friend, who was buying the donuts, was taken out of context, and I am sorry for not using more discretion with my choice of words.'

Continuing, she said: 'As an advocate for healthy eating, food is very important to me and I sometimes get upset by how freely we as Americans eat and consume things without giving any thought to the consequences that it has on our health and society as a whole. The fact that the United States has one of the highest child obesity rates in the world frustrates me. We need to do more to educate ourselves and our children about the dangers of overeating and the poison that we put into our bodies.'

She also recorded a video for YouTube, to put her thoughts out directly to the world, feeling that this route was the best chance she had of avoiding her words being misrepresented. 'I just wanted to make a video to apologize again for the whole donut fiasco and craziness because I feel like the apology I posted, I kind of missed my opportunity to actually sincerely apologize and express how I was feeling, because I was too busy preaching about my issues with the food industry, which is not, I feel like, relative.' She went on to address her comment in the shop about hating Americans as she explained: 'I've actually never been prouder to be an American to be honest with you. The advances that we've made in the past couple months and all the wonderful progressive things that have been going on. Never been prouder of this country actually.'

She then turned to explain that the incident was a 'rude awakening' after seeing the video of incident. 'I was so disgusted with myself, I like wanted to shove my face into a pillow and like disappear, but instead of that I'm going to come forward and own up to what I did and take responsibility and say I'm sorry.'

What a saga it turned into though! It was even featured on *The Muppet Show*, where the Swedish Chef character parodied the incident. Miley Cyrus referenced it in a rendition of 'My Way', on *Saturday Night Live*. Later, Ariana decided that if it was good enough for Miley it was good enough for her, and nodded to it during her own *Saturday Night Live* slot. She said that she wanted an 'adult scandal' and asked 'What will my scandal be?'

Then there were further apologies from Ariana, who found it hard to shake off the 'scandal', even as time passed. 'My behavior was very offensive and I apologized. There's no excuse, or there's nothing to justify it, but I think that as human beings we all say and do things that we don't mean at all sometimes, and we have to learn from it,' she told *Good Morning America* two months later. 'I mean that's part of our process. We have to learn from our mistakes – that's how we grow.'

Scooter Braun, never a manager to eschew the limelight himself, explained in the *New York Times* how he saw the incident and what he had said about it to Ariana. 'I tell her, you have to address the mistakes that you made and own them,' he said. 'Some of the words she used in that shop were things she needed to address, and she did. But I also think – not about her, but just in general – we're getting a little ridiculous when it comes to donuts and eggs … Let's talk about some real stuff. Why are we discussing that when we have real significant issues in the world? Like, gun control. And the fact that a presidential candidate is saying things that I find to be anti-American. These are the things we should be angry and frustrated about.'

However, the ripples continued. Before long, there was a political dimension to the saga. Among thousands of emails from the Democratic National

Committee (DNC) that were posted on WikiLeaks was one concerning Ariana and the scandal. 'Ariana Butera – video caught her licking other peoples' donuts while saying she hates America,' the DNC's deputy compliance director wrote in response, referring to Grande by her real name. 'Republican Congressman used this video and said it was a double standard that liberals were not upset with her like they are with Trump who criticized Mexicans; cursed out a person on Twitter after that person used an offensive word towards her brother.'

Misspelling her name, he asked: 'Can we also vet Arianna Grande?' Turning to her apologies, the email continues: 'In the second of her two YouTube apologies posted last week, the twenty-two-year-old singer said she was "disgusted" with herself and wanted to "disappear" after TMZ posted the video.'

Republican Congressman Jeff Duncan also weighed in with a lengthy Facebook post, which criticized America's 'double standards' in letting Grande get away with bashing the country while holding Donald Trump accountable for controversial things he had said. 'This misguided young pop star said that she hated America and hated Americans, while she proceeded to contaminate food for resale with the very tongue with which she uttered the hatred rant,' Duncan wrote. 'The double-standards in this country are disgusting.'

Doughnut-gate proved to be something Ariana was unable to leave behind. For some people, the name

Ariana Grande was now less synonymous with her music, and more connected with doughnuts – which was not a position she had ever expected to be in. At the 2016 MTV VMAs, American radio host Charlamagne Tha God brought up the topic, saying: 'Now you can't go around licking no pastries tonight.' Ariana looked surprised. 'OK, I'll take notes,' she said. 'I'll keep it in mind.' She kept her calm and focused on the evening's more pertinent dimension: she was nominated for five VMAs: Best Female Video, Best Collaboration, Best Pop Video, Best Cinematography and Best Editing.

At least *Vanity Fair* saw the lighter side of the story, with a tongue-in-cheek take on it. 'Ariana Grande has become death, the destroyer of worlds,' it said, paraphrasing a line from the Hindu scripture *Bhagavad Gita*, adding: 'Or, at least, the potential destroyer of doughnut shops.' It continued in a similarly sarcastic tone: 'I mean, licking goddamned doughnuts and then speaking ill of America and her beautiful peoples? That's some peculiar, unsettling behavior. But what demonic motive could be behind all this?' It added that 'Satan' had 'dispatched a minion' in Ariana.

Actress Susan Sarandon, too, used humour to try to puncture the pomposity. 'Today, lick a doughnut in solidarity with @ArianaGrande,' she wrote on Twitter. 'A sweet, talented, true American.' In response to the actress's intervention, *Vanity Fair* asked: 'Does this mean Susan Sarandon is guided by the same hellish hand? What is going on here?' Richard Lawson wrapped up his sardonic article by writing: 'I choose to believe that all of our fates dance on the tip of Ariana Grande's tongue, that we are all mere pawns in this tiny titan's game of oblivion.' Ariana might well have laughed at this article, which supported her with just the sort of sarcastic humour she enjoys.

Indeed, reluctantly joking along with the moment was the best she could do. For Ariana, it was time to accept that, for the time being at least, the doughnut shadow was going to remain cast over her. The best thing she could do was crack on with what she did best – making sweet music. She was about to do that, but amid the sweetness there was an element of darkness. Ariana had grown up – and her third album would reflect that.

CHAPTER NINE

THIRD TIME'S THE CHARM

Pop albums can be great documents of where their artist is in their life – particularly for younger artists. Between *Yours Truly* and its successor, Ariana had grown up, and the works reflected that. She wanted an even bigger step upwards with her third album. That was the message she laid out loud and clear when she began recording work on it in 2015. With her love of the studio life, she was thrilled to get back in there. With a collection of songs she was proud of, she could hardly wait to hit the studio and begin to develop them – and then get recording.

The question was, where she would find the time for it? Given her hectic schedule, initially she had to slot in studio sessions among her other work, including live performances. During the summer and autumn of

2015, she squeezed in recording time between her tour dates and other commitments. She did the bulk of the recording work at MXM Studios in Los Angeles and Wolf Cousins Studios in Stockholm, Sweden.

Ariana worked with a team of producers and executives, including familiar faces such as Max Martin and Savan Kotecha. On MTV she said of her rehiring of Martin: 'He's like a mathematician. He knows music like math. It just makes sense to him.' She was also joined by friends with guest appearances by Nicki Minaj, Lil Wayne, Macy Gray and Future. Macy Gray was full of praise for Ariana. At forty-eight, Gray was more than old enough to be Ariana's mother. So her verdict made Ariana smile. 'She's a pure singer,' Gray told *Hello!* magazine. 'It's similar to what Mariah Carey, Whitney Houston and Christina Aguilera have – that power thing. But I didn't realize that. She does all these pop records where you can get a song across without showing your chops.'

Initially, Ariana hinted that the album would be called *Moonlight*. During a conversation on Twitter, one of her fans asked, '"Moonlight" is a new song? Or the name of the new album?' To which Ariana responded, 'Both.' But then she changed her mind, as she explained during a television interview on *Jimmy Kimmel Live*. 'A really long time ago I was convinced that the album was going to be called *Moonlight* because it was one of my favourite songs that'd we done,' she said. 'Now, as we're wrapping things up, I've been writing and singing

… and there's this other song that has thrown me for a whirlwind. I don't know, I love it so much and it changed everything. "Moonlight" is a lovely song … It's really romantic, and it definitely ties together the old music and the new music. But "Dangerous Woman" is a lot stronger.'

Less than six months after the final single from *My Everything* was released, she kicked off excitement for the new collection, embarking on a thirty-day countdown on Instagram to the album's lead single. She did publicity stunts across other platforms, too, ever the sassy, canny operator. Taking to YouTube, she told her adoring fans: 'What I came here to do in this world is not only to entertain but to love, to share, to listen, to improve, to learn, to share music, to share experience, to share feelings, to make people feel happy and empowered.' Taking an ever more spiritual tone, she continued: 'When I say "focus on me" I'm not asking to be the center of attention. I'm not asking you to focus on my face or my clothes or my body or my singing voice. By "focus on me", I literally mean focus on me. Focus on what I'm all about and what I believe in.' Given her study of the Kabbalah, this angle was far from unexpected. As we have seen, Madonna took the spiritual truths she had learned at the Kabbalah Center and tried to blend them into her music, and into the lives of her listeners and fans. Ariana, similarly, wanted to elevate her message.

But it was still, at heart, a pop album, and Ariana

remained, essentially, a pop star. As such, she wanted to get into racier, more grown-up territory, and see how she felt in there. Perhaps she may even enjoy the slightly darker plains? 'The album is definitely the next step for me,' she told Ryan Seacrest. 'It still sounds like me, but it feels like a more mature, evolved version. There's a nice blend of the R&B vibes and a nice blend of pop vibes. The whole body of work is a little darker and sexier and more mature.' As we will see, she succeeded in this aim.

A new courage and self-confidence was growing inside of Ariana, and she was ready to let it out in the studio for this new album. 'I want it to be strong and empowering because I've come into my own a little bit,' she told the *Daily Telegraph*. 'Whereas before, I think I was afraid to be myself and make decisions and speak out about things I'm passionate about because I thought it would make me experience some of the stereotypes that women in power often face.'

We can also draw insights into the thinking and emotion behind the project from Ariana's brother, Frankie. Talking to Bustle, he said: 'I think it pushed her in a different direction with her album where she was allowing that inner, dangerous woman to come out.' Expanding on his point, he added: 'It's also a celebration of everyone's dangerous woman. There's a dangerous woman inside of you and you can choose to let her out. You can choose to not let her out … That's the point –

feminism means you get to choose. And that's what the whole album is: her making very strong decisions.'

So what were the results of those very strong decisions? Would her third album herald a new dawn for Ariana, in which she showcased her strength of mind? There was only one way to find out. The album begins with its one-time title track, 'Moonlight'. This soaring ballad was very clearly inspired by the music of the 1950s – and Ariana rendered it very well. It was correctly described by Digital Spy as a 'twinkly production', which makes the song sound 'like it was composed among the fluffy clouds in the sky'. It is a magnificent, old-fashioned song, and a very fitting opener – its old-school style lulls the listener into thinking that the whole collection ahead of them might hark back to times past.

But that's not the case. From what might have been the title track to what actually became the title track: the second song is 'Dangerous Woman'. This is a decidedly modern and sultry tune. The guitar track is positively raunchy and the beat is seductive. Then comes the voice: Ariana is imperious and Rihanna-like. She sounds like that pop princess did on her *Rated R* album. The 'somethin' bout, somethin' bout' refrain is infectious, an early sign that this album is going to be rammed with addictive vocal hooks. This song is Ariana on majestic form, a true pop queen for our times. The moment you hear it on the album you cannot wait to hear it live.

Track three is 'Be Alright' – and that is just what the listener is as they take in this confident, sassy triumph. It is a summery deep house tune, which takes the over-familiar standards of Ibiza parties and transports them to a more sophisticated and original place. Rather than being yet another cheap, hands-in-the-air cliché, it is instead a more measured affair. Despite these stylistic subtleties, however, the song still leaves you in the ecstatic realms of the Ibiza standard. It has just taken a different, somewhat more chilled, route to get you there. The xylophone notes that open and close it add a nice touch.

Then comes 'Into You', which is a stunning work, notable for many reasons, not least because Ariana manages to channel and quote both Elvis Presley and Mariah Carey in a single clause. Then there are the trio of wonders that are the cheeky synths, the booming club beat, lurking synths and the cool clicks. The chorus grabs you by the throat and won't let it go until you're bopping and singing along to its glory. It won't need to wait long. This time the refrain is 'into you, into you, into you …' At this point the album is still in its early stages, and yet it has already delivered some glorious earworm moments. One reviewer said that 'Into You' is 'as close to perfection as possible'. Praise cannot get higher than that, and it is also worth noting how Ariana's vocals are deeper than usual here.

Then pop legend Nicki Minaj shows up for 'Side to

Side', giving the album a change of pace in so many senses. Musically, it moves from the nightclub to reggae on the beach. The darkness of the album also really begins to kick in here, with Ariana singing about doing a deal with the Devil. This sort of lyrical content would have been absolutely unimaginable on *Yours Truly*, and at the very least rather incongruous on *My Everything*.

As Minaj exits another guest arrives – Lil Wayne is in the house for 'Let Me Love You'. But the air remains just as x-rated, as Ariana sings about looking for her next conquest, just as one is finishing. The very presence of Wayne does, of course, lend the song a dark side all of its own. 'Greedy' is described by Digital Spy as 'a shiny disco-pop number with a groove so infectious the World Health Organization would have good grounds to label it an epidemic'. A disco-flavoured, key-changing, uptempo joy, it is another triumph. It has a retro feel and yet its feet are planted firmly in the twenty-first century. 'Everyday', featuring Future, is a solid R&B effort, with the now familiar feature of chorus vocals being given by a female act to a male rapper. Again, there is an addictive chorus, a simple refrain of 'everyday, everyday, everyday'. It's such a satisfying track and again explores new terrain, living up to Ariana's promises that she would show us a new side of her, a truer side of her, on the album. Her falsetto vocals are so on point.

It is only when we arrive at the mellowed-out 'Sometimes', that the Ariana who listeners know from previous albums reappears. This is the Ariana of her early years, with her and a guitar forming the bulk of the sound, in sharp contrast to the noisier, fuller productions elsewhere on the album. Long-standing fans get a chance to relive those times, whereas newcomers get a hint of where she came from. Although the track is less in-your-face than others on the album, that understated nature does not mean it is less than impressive. The album has, by now, become due for something of a different intensity, and 'Sometimes' delivers it. It is flirty and sweet, as she looks back with maturity and perspective on a relationship that did not work out. This is a good message for her fans to remember when they face life's inevitable heartbreaks and hardships.

Trident Media summed up the song with accurate panache when it declared: 'Imagine you're on a beach. It's sunset, you're with your friends, you have a fire going, it's very chilled out, and you're drinking (responsibly). Someone's brought their speakers. This would be the song to play.' If someone has yet to play 'Sometimes' in such circumstances, then it is high time they did.

One of the album's more experimental turns comes on 'I Don't Care'. A reviewer for Andpop wrote that the song is 'Ariana at her most honest. It represents her refusal to let what others say get to her. We love a woman that isn't afraid to be herself.' Musically, it sounds at once like an old-fashioned cinematic score and a twenty-first-century R&B classic. Where some of the album's tracks are instant classics, this one is more of a grower, needing repeated plays before its worth is truly appreciated. Its Hollywood tinge sits a little incongruously on *Dangerous Woman*. It is such a gentle effort that it is easy to drift into other thoughts as you listen – but that is not something that can be said about its successor, 'Bad Decisions'. A hip-hop bouncer, it is yet another instant, infectious and lively classic. Some fans have speculated that this song's title is a nod to the doughnut scandal, and the way Ariana asks whether listeners have ever seen a princess be a 'bad bitch' would add weight to that theory. Lyrically, this is one of the album's strongest songs. The Nickelodeon years have never felt further away – but the Mariah Carey comparisons that Ariana so often attracts are spot on.

'Touch It' is another edgy moment. The grimy bassline alone is worth digging into this song. Although the song's subject matter is one of frustration and unhappiness over unrequited passion, Ariana takes this negative emotion to a positive place with her assured delivery. She is tired of being patient in waiting for the big moment and she is desperate for the phone to ring. So many listeners will have been in just that place and it is wonderful that Ariana gave them this anthem to help them through it.

'Nobody Like Me' and 'Forever Boy' are melded into one track. The former is an R&B tune, which starts with staccato keys before Ariana sings about seeing straight through a man. Then comes the second song, which is housey and a considerable step upwards. With Balearic percussion and happy words, this EDM beauty packs a really uplifting chorus.

'Thinking Bout You' concerns the throes of a complicated relationship. Ariana sings of being hung up on a man during his absence. She cannot have the man physically with her in the moment but she has, and obsesses over, her memories of him. A marvellously produced effort, it has breathy vocals, an eventual heavy beat and amazing atmosphere. You can imagine it forming part of the soundtrack on a romantic-comedy series or feelgood film. Some claimed that this track felt like a filler, rather than a climactic final bang, yet for others the way it blends both sadness and joy is remarkable – a fitting end to a bold album.

What an astonishing and confident collection it proved to be. But what would the critics think? Music reviewers are notoriously hard to please, after all. This time, in the UK, *The Observer*, which had previously been less than complimentary about Ariana's material, was impressed. Michael Cragg gave the album four out of five stars, and described it as a refinement of her sound. He singled out the title track, 'Everyday' and 'Moonlight' for particular praise. Summing up the collection in general, he wrote: 'Held together by Grande's skyscraping voice, *Dangerous Woman* throws a lot at the wall and, brilliantly, most of it sticks.'

British music weekly *NME*, which has historically been extremely hostile – sneering, even – to young pop acts, was also praising. Larry Bartleet said the album carried 'a message of empowerment that rings true'. He added that 'it's not only the consistent songwriting clout that elevates this album from recent efforts by Grande's teen-star peers, Demi Lovato and Selena Gomez'. He said its 'modish message of empowerment feels honest coming from Grande', referring to the content of the essay she had written on the topic.

Sputnik Music published an epic review, describing *Dangerous Woman* as 'one of the year's best pop albums'. However, it also delivered a few punches, arguing that while '*Dangerous Woman* remains one of this year's most intriguing pop releases', it 'also suggests that Ariana Grande may never reach that upper echelon, as she once again finds herself bound by her loyalty to genre clichés that sell and an inability to string together one totally cohesive album'. These were not knockout blows but they were blows, all the same.

Andpop's Rebecca Mattina wrote: 'If there's anything we can take from *Dangerous Woman*, it's that she's growing as an artist.' Mattina continued, 'It's part throwback fun, part sultry and sexy, and we are obsessed.' Playing on the album's title, she summed her verdict up by saying: 'There's no danger in snatching up this record.'

AllMusic gave *Dangerous Woman* four out of five stars. 'Restraint serves her well: there are times she lets go with a full-throated roar, but Grande spends most of *Dangerous Woman* at a simmer that reinforces the sultry seduction of the title,' wrote Stephen Thomas Erlewine. He continued that 'a fair chunk of the album is devoted to cinematic ballads, which makes the bright blasts of disco … so alluring, but the entire record benefits from this single-minded concentration'. He enjoyed the collection's 'sly, subtle distinctions – a little bit of torch gives way to some heavy hip only to have frothy pop surface again – and while some of these cuts work better than others, the range is impressive, as is Grande's measured, assured performance'.

Entertainment Weekly's Nolan Feeney said that 'While the hooks may not be as irresistible as her 2014 double whammy of "Problem" and "Break Free", Grande compensates by having something meaningful to say with that jaw-dropping voice – one of the most exquisite in pop today.' Feeney gave *Dangerous Woman* a B+ and concluded: 'For Grande, giving up on pleasing everybody has only made her more magnetic.'

Slant magazine gave *Dangerous Woman* three and a half stars out of five. Sal Cinquemani felt the album was in two halves: she enjoyed the first half but felt it then became 'limited' by 'strict adherence to contemporary pop and R&B trends'. She consequently singled out for praise the minimalist deep-house banger 'Be Alright' and the impeccably produced 'Let Me Love You', and the way 'Macy Gray channels Nina Simone on "Leave Me Lonely"', and Ariana's 'coy, youthful performance on the disco-funk "Greedy"'.

Spin magazine was more negative. Affording the album just six out of ten stars, Theon Weber said that at its best, the album's tracks suggested a 'strong persona – haughty, insatiable, a little manic, really into you'. However, elsewhere the 'edges are softened and her weird intensity diminished'. *Rolling Stone*, too, was less than blown away, complaining that 'her talents are wasted on meaningful-sounding but ultimately trite lyrics'.

But the overall chorus from the critical community was positive, as exemplified by Lewis Corner from Digital Spy, who wrote that Grande 'ultimately pulled together a consistent collection that impressively manages to keep your attention over fifteen tracks', and *USA Today*'s Maeve McDermott, who said that it is 'a mature portrait of an artist blessed with one of pop's strongest voices, brimming with potential hits'.

For Ariana, the making of the album, and preparations for its release, were a time of turmoil because of a change she made in her management set-up. In February 2016, she parted ways with Scooter Braun, after concluding that things were not working well for her any longer. Denying suggestions that she had fallen out with Braun's crown jewel, Justin Bieber, a source told *Star* magazine: 'Ariana always has and continues to support Justin.' Instead, added the source, she did not think the relationship was 'working for her professionally anymore' and it was therefore 'time to move on'.

She continued to work with the line-up at Untitled Entertainment, including manager Stephanie Simon, whom Ariana had known for many years. Significantly, joining the managerial line-up for Ariana was her mother Joan. However, Scooter Braun was back in the fold within months. In September, reports surfaced that Braun was seen accompanying Grande to recent tapings of *The Tonight Show* and was back in charge.

Ariana embarked on a busy set of media slots to promote the album and in doing so noticed that, with each new release, the level of interest in her from the print and broadcast media rose. For *Dangerous Woman*, it rocketed. The peak of the promotional tour came when she appeared on *Saturday Night Live*, on which she delivered a knowing monologue, which touched on some of her recent controversies. 'It can be tough growing up in show business, you know?' she said. 'A lot of kid stars end up doing drugs, or in jail, or pregnant, or get caught looking at a doughnut they didn't pay for … Which, yes, was childish and stupid … [but] I think I'm in a place where I'm ready to be caught in a real adult scandal,' she continued, before launching into a jazzy showtune called 'What Will My Scandal Be?'

She did an impersonation of Britney Spears,

brilliantly mimicking her curious vocal style on 'One More Time', before taking off Shakira equally well. Asked if she could impersonate Ariana Grande, she declined, joking: 'Sorry, not a big fan.' When it came to Rihanna, Ariana not only had the vocals down to a tee, but also mocked her movements with ease. Her Celine Dion was also magnificent. Luckily, Celine Dion saw the funny side of it – and then some: she said she 'peed herself' watching the mimicry.

Later, Ariana poked fun at the 'regular person' image that actress Jennifer Lawrence espouses, saying: 'They told me not to do a game show, but I was like, "Screw it, I can have fun, I'm a regular person."' In a subsequent interview, Lawrence commented on the impersonation. The *Hunger Games* star described it as 'Spot-f***ing-on' – but added that she would never label herself a 'regular person'. Lawrence insisted: 'That's what other people have said. If I'd said, "I'm a regular person", I'd want to kill myself.'

But it was Ariana's Whitney Houston that was the best, when she sang 'I Will Always Love You'. The camera cropped in tight to her face as she nailed the song's big chorus. For a moment, she was back in her childhood, when she first fell in love with Houston, and sang along to her tracks in her bedroom.

She got the chance to perform with one of her other idols when she appeared on stage at Madonna's Raising Malawi fundraiser show during the international art fair, Art Basel, at Faena Forum in Miami. Ariana helped to raise over $7.5 million for the Raising Malawi Foundation, which 'addresses the poverty and hardship endured by Malawi's orphans and vulnerable children' by partnering with local organizations to provide Malawian children and their caregivers with critical resources.

That appearance came during rehearsals for her next production: *Hairspray Live*. Alongside Jennifer Hudson, Ariana went down a storm in NBC's holiday musical production. A three-hour telecast saw NBC triumphantly stage the 1962-set musical inspired by John Waters' 1988 movie.

The end of 2016 also saw Ariana appear on Stevie Wonder's single 'Faith', which was the lead single from the soundtrack of the 2016 musical-animated film *Sing* and was subsequently nominated for Best Original Song at the Seventy-Fourth Golden Globe Awards. They performed it at the grand finale of the US reality series *The Voice*. As *Hollywood Life* put it: 'What do you get when you put Stevie Wonder and Ariana Grande on the same stage? You get one epic performance.'

With the media promotional junket for *Dangerous Woman* completed, and these sideshows over, it was time for Ariana to prepare to tour. Tickets went on sale on 20 September 2016, with the tour itself beginning on 3 February 2017, in Phoenix, Arizona, then moving on to other dates in North America, Europe, Latin

America, Asia and Oceania. Little could anyone have known at this stage what a painful tragedy would strike at one of the dates.

Victoria Monét and Little Mix were hooked in as opening support acts for the American dates, while rapper BIA joined for the fateful UK leg. Ariana's stylist Law Roach and designer Bryan Hearns put their heads together to fashion a more 'mature' onstage look for Ariana. As Hearns put it in *InStyle* magazine: 'It's about making an adult Ariana, marrying her silhouette with what's happening in fashion right now, so a big theme is sportswear – everything is oversized, there are straps everywhere, and cool hardware ... It's definitely more edgy, it's more adult, but still playful and young.'

Some of the preparations for her onstage look were made at the last moment, which put Hearns right on the seat of his pants the evening before the first date. 'I slept for four hours. It was stressful, but it was exciting. It was awesome, he told *Hollywood Reporter*: 'Most of the looks are my direct aesthetic, so I put my stamp on it. It was just a certain silhouette that she wanted and certain colors, and that's how we met in the middle. We had a couple of looks that were in her silhouette, which is usually high-waisted bodysuits, shorts, skirts and crop tops. It's very flattering on her so we have a lot of items in that shape.'

There were four separate chapters, or acts, to the show. The opening one began ten minutes before Ariana took to the stage. A countdown time is projected on to the screen, at the end of which she emerges with a group of ten dancers. She opened with 'Be Alright', then came 'Everyday', the latter accompanied by pyrotechnics, and guest Future singing his track remotely via the video screen. This segment was closed by 'Let Me Love You'.

When Ariana appeared for the second chapter, she was dressed in white. She sang 'Knew Better', 'Forever Boy', 'One Last Time' and 'Touch It', to the delight of the audience. With video and lighting effects aplenty, and Ariana taking to the elevated platform, this was a dramatic segment of the show. For the third act, there was a clear message. In the preliminary video intro, a series of empowering, feminist terms were projected on the screen: 'empowered', 'strong', 'grounded', 'connected', 'not asking for it' (which repeats multiple times), 'free', 'soulful', 'divine', among several others. The third act took in such bangers as 'Side to Side', 'Greedy', 'Focus' and 'I Don't Care'. In the fourth act, which saw Ariana decked out in a white bra and harem pants, she belted out some of her biggest hits and most crowd-pleasing classics. Here came 'Moonlight', 'Love Me Harder', 'Break Free' and 'Sometimes'. She then added 'Problem' and 'Into You', before encoring with 'Dangerous Woman'. The backing band continued an instrumental of the song after Ariana left the stage, playing the audience into the night.

After her date in Las Vegas, the *Las Vegas Weekly* published a five-pronged review of the show. Ian

Caramanzana wrote that, in addition to the expected tweens and children in the audience, there were 'middle-aged couples, older gents in suits and younger groups dressed like it's a hot nightclub pre-game event'. These were just the sort of more mature fans that Ariana had hoped she would begin to attract with the tone of material she put on *Dangerous Woman*.

'Like a true diva, Grande drinks her bottled water through a straw,' Caramanzana continued. Turning to the music itself, he said Ariana's 'burly, soulful vibrato and wide range remain the star of her show, and she's at her best when it's just her, a microphone and her band'. When the tour rolled through the Big Apple, Ariana made what was seen as a political comment in response to a controversial move by President Donald Trump: 'It might seem to be a scary time to be yourself', she said, adding: 'You're beautiful and your differences are beautiful.' As she crooned 'Thinking Bout You', the video screen behind her showed silhouettes of loving couples, encompassing a range of gender combinations. The fact that this came the day after Trump's White House revoked guidelines protecting transgender students for using bathrooms of their choice was not lost on many.

Jon Pareles of the *New York Times* wrote that it was a 'show of confidence, prowess and aplomb'. He added: 'Ariana Grande asserts herself by acting like she doesn't have to.' The *Washington Post* wrote that Ariana 'held her own as a dancer – despite impossibly high heels

– hip-rolling and bunny-hopping across the runway-reminiscent stage'. However, their writer Chris Kelly had a significant technical issue with the show: 'Her gorgeous four-octave soprano was often obscured by her bass-heavy backing band.' Dan Hyman of the *Chicago Tribune* also had issues, writing that 'aside from a massive projection screen that lived behind the stage and stretched the width of the arena, the production seemed a bit cheap for a show of this scale'.

In Britain, Kitty Empire of *The Guardian* was also critical, though looked at from a different angle, her criticism carried a backhanded compliment within it. 'Grande's constant state of climax stretches credulity,' she wrote after watching a UK date. '"One Last Time" is a love song set at the end of the world. The thunderous production and her multiple climaxes make sense here. But Grande yelps at anything. If you asked "tea or coffee?", she would cough up a kaleidoscope. Inquire about sugar and she would vomit unicorns.'

As with her album releases, the two critics whom Ariana most wanted to please did not work for newspapers or music websites. Those two critics were her fans and herself. If her fans were thrilled that meant more to her than pleasing critics twice her age. She also wanted to be proud herself, of what she had done.

Given what happened on 22 May 2017 and the impact it had on Ariana, it is worth pausing here to take a scan of where she was in her life and career at this stage.

At twenty-three years of age, she had achieved what felt like several lifetimes of accomplishments. Having first trod the theatrical boards at the age of eight, she starred in local productions of *Annie* and *The Wizard of Oz*. Meanwhile, she had learned the French horn and written songs inspired by artists such as the DIY indie act Imogen Heap. As she tried out singing, she discovered she had quite a vocal range: she could reach four octaves with ease and skill. This self-described 'very weird little girl' would soon take this vocal ability and love of performance and conquer the world. Having grabbed the role of Charlotte in the Broadway production of *13: The Musical* and then taken on Cat Valentine on the Nickelodeon sitcom *Victorious* and its spin-off, *Sam & Cat*, she was well on the way by her mid-teens.

Her first single 'Put Your Hearts Up', might not have been one that she enjoyed particularly or later stood by, but it propelled her to just where she wanted to be – under the spotlight in the pop music world. There, she could release her album, including material she was far prouder of, such as 'The Way', and then the track which really reflected her whims, the magnificent 'Problem'.

Although allegations of diva behaviour and the doughnut scandal proved obstacles on the way, Ariana continued to blaze a trail. For every critical headline there was a personal triumph, including her increasingly opinionated position on issues such as bullying, misogyny and gender identification. She became almost a spokeswoman for a generation of young women, but this did not mean she had forgotten about the music: her third album *Dangerous Woman* went platinum in the US and gold in the UK, spawned a trio of top 10 hits and a Grammy nomination for best pop album.

Then, one night in May 2017, she took to the stage in Manchester. She had recently played in Dublin, Birmingham and Amsterdam. She was excited for the Manchester shows, with shows in London and Belgium also on the horizon. By this stage, nearly four months into the tour, she was well drilled in the production. Just days before, a reviewer for the Manchester show had observed the joy of the 'cat-ear-sporting pre-teens' who made up much of the audience and the 'relentless ejaculations' of Ariana's vocals. She took a deep breath, sauntered on to the stage and then gave it her all during the four acts of the show. At the end of the gig, she thanked the audience and left the stage. Hundreds of pink balloons were released. Then something happened that would horrify the planet.

CHAPTER TEN

TRAGEDY AND TERROR

What had been another evening show on another tour became the hardest night of Ariana Grande's life. She stepped off the stage, and then, at 10.31 p.m., tragedy and terror struck as suicide bomber Salman Ramadan Abedi detonated a shrapnel-stuffed home-made bomb at the exit of the Manchester venue. The explosive was crammed with nuts, bolts and nails, to maximize its deadly impact. The audience, more than 14,000 strong in number, were the targets. Kids, friends on a night out they had saved up for, and counted down the days towards. Innocents, not as unintentional 'collateral damage' but as the specific target. Even in an age of terror, this was a particularly wicked act.

As concertgoers fled in abject panic they were

confronted by a scene from hell: bodies strewn across the floor. By 10.35 p.m. the emergency services were speeding to the venue in response to reports of an explosion. The first doctor believed to have been on the scene was an off-duty consultant anaesthetist, Dr Michael Daley. The police declared a 'serious incident' at 10.55 p.m. and just under an hour later they confirmed there had been a number of deaths. 'This is currently being treated as a terrorist incident until the police know otherwise,' the Manchester police said on Twitter. The wounded were taken to eight hospitals around the city.

Ariana was backstage. At first there was confusion as to what had happened. Then, as the ghastly picture became clearer, she and her crew fell to pieces. Joan had still been sitting in her front row seat at the Manchester Arena, waiting to go backstage to see Ariana, when the bomb went off. Eyewitnesses reported that, as the panic began, Joan called around ten young fans to follow her backstage, where she and members of her security team took care of them until they could leave the venue safely.

Meanwhile, parents waiting to collect their daughters stood confused at first, as droves of young fans fled the venue in tears, with screams filling the air. Young fans often cry and scream with excitement when they see their heroes in the flesh so, at least at first, some parents thought the emotional outpouring was merely that. Even the noise of the explosion could have been misunderstood outside the venue; considered a concert pyrotechnic rather than a bomb. Then, sensing the intensity and panic of the outbursts, the parents realized something dreadful had happened.

The eyewitnesses who had seen that dreadful thing first-hand gave horrific and graphic, if understandably somewhat confused, accounts. A concertgoer called Sarah described the chaotic, panicked scenes as people tried to flee the scene. She told Radio Manchester: 'I heard the explosion. Everyone was shoving and pushing. There were so many little kids in there. I couldn't get out and there were crowds of people blocking everywhere.' Soon, the scene was more like a war zone than a pop concert. 'By the time I got outside there were so many people crying and standing in the road,' Sarah continued. 'It was absolute chaos. I saw people covered in blood. I have never been in a situation like this before.'

Nineteen-year-old Ryan Morrison was walking through the Arena when he heard the loud explosion. Speaking to the *Manchester Evening News*, he recalled: 'It was one massive bang and then I saw smoke. I heard someone shout "bomb" and then everyone started running. It was carnage. People were injured by being trampled as they tried to get out. It was absolute carnage.' He added: 'They were running through the streets, people were confused and trying to find their friends. They were crying. It was like something out of a film. It was surreal.'

Gary Walker, from Leeds, was waiting with his wife in the foyer. He told the BBC: 'We heard the last song, and quite a few people were flooding out and then suddenly there was a massive flash and then a bang and smoke. I felt a bit of pain in my foot and my leg. My wife said, "I need to lie down". I lay her down, she'd got a stomach wound and possibly a broken leg. I was about three metres from the actual explosion.'

Another concertgoer, Sasina Akhtar, told the *Manchester Evening News* that there had been an explosion at the back of the arena after the last song. 'We saw young girls with blood on them,' she said. 'Everyone was screaming, and people were running.' Karen Ford told the BBC: 'Everyone was just getting out of their seats and walking toward the stairs when all of a sudden a huge sound, which sounded like an explosion, went off … Everyone tried to push people up the stairs,' she remembered, adding that amid the chaos, people tried to push past a woman in a wheelchair as children screamed.

She said there was no smoke, just one really loud bang. 'It was very, very loud,' she said, adding that her husband thought he had heard a second explosion. 'There were shoes on the floor left behind by people who had fled,' she recalled. 'I was trying to tell people to calm down … We were being crushed.'

Photographs of the aftermath painted the same picture. Debris and casualties in the foyer area of the arena. Metal nuts and bolts were strewn around the floor among bodies. More than 240 emergency calls were made; sixty ambulances and 400 police officers attended. The nearby Victoria train station was quickly closed, leaving many without a way to get home. Showing the good side of human nature, residents of Manchester mobilized and offered free transport and accommodation to those who needed it. What a contrast to those behind the attack. Parents separated from their children during the bedlam were told to report to a Holiday Inn, where many fans had been offered refuge. A number of other hotels opened their doors to concertgoers trapped inside the police cordon, providing them with drinks and phone chargers to enable them to contact family members. The four nearby Sikh temples - Sri Guru Gobind Singh Gurdwara Educational and Cultural Centre, Gurdwara Sri Guru Harkrisham Sahib, Dasmesh Sikh Temple and Central Gurdwara Manchester – all kept their doors open for victims throughout the night.

The following morning, Britain woke up to the shocking news. Indeed, the atrocity became a top news story around the world. Soon, politicians began to respond. 'All acts of terrorism are cowardly attacks on innocent people, but this attack stands out for its appalling, sickening cowardice, deliberately targeting innocent, defenceless children and young people who should have been enjoying one of the most memorable nights of their lives,' said Prime Minister Theresa May. The leader of the opposition, Jeremy Corbyn, said he was 'horrified by the horrendous events in Manchester'. Two days later, hundreds of people gathered in Manchester city centre to observe a minute's silence to remember the victims of the Arena bomb attack.

After the attack, the UK terrorism threat level was raised from 'severe' to 'critical' for the first time since 2007. This change indicated that another attack was imminently expected. Members of the armed forces replaced armed police at certain 'key sites'. The attacker was soon named as twenty-two-year-old Salman Abedi. He was one of three siblings and was born in Manchester on New Year's Eve, 1994. The family, of Libyan origin, lived at several properties in Manchester, including homes that were raided by police. He went to the Burnage Academy for Boys in Manchester between 2009 and 2011, before going to The Manchester College until 2013 and then Salford University in 2014. According to the BBC, members of the public called an anti-terrorism hotline after Abedi had been heard expressing the views that 'he was supporting terrorism' and 'being a suicide bomber was OK', though these reports have been disputed. Abedi had been arrested for minor offences in 2012 but was not known to the government's *Prevent* Strategy.

What of Ariana herself amid all this chaos and trauma? TMZ reported that she was inconsolable and 'in hysterics'. Her first official statement was to write on Twitter that she was 'broken'. She added: 'from the bottom of my heart, i am so so sorry. i don't have words.' For some months, this became the most liked tweet in history. Her manager Scooter Braun, said on Twitter, 'We mourn the lives of children and loved ones taken by this cowardly act.'

Ariana immediately suspended the tour and flew home to Florida. *US Weekly* reported that she was greeted by her family and her boyfriend, Mac Miller, at an airport near her home town of Boca Raton. 'Mac ran up to give her a hug and kiss right after her plane landed,' an eyewitness said.

In the days that followed, the true toll of the attack became clear: twenty-three adults and children were killed, including the attacker Abedi, and 250 were injured. Those killed included ten people aged under twenty. The youngest victim was an eight-year-old girl called Saffie Roussos, and the oldest was a fifty-one-year-old woman. Elaine McIver, an off-duty police officer, was also among those killed. She was with her partner, Paul, and two children, all of whom were injured.

The Islamic State of Iraq and the Levant, also known as ISIS or Islamic State, announced through the Nashir Telegram channel that the attack was carried out by 'a soldier of the Khilafah'. It said the bombing was 'an endeavour to terrorize the *mushrikin*, and in response to their transgressions against the lands of the Muslims'. The attacker's sister said she believed he might have been motivated by revenge for Muslim children killed by American air strikes in Syria.

In time, Ariana released a longer response, in the form of a letter that was so fitting in tone, so eloquent and healing. This was not a brief, vacuous statement rushed out by a celebrity and their team. It felt bigger and better than that – a heartfelt and genuine passage, full of emotion and sincerity, yet also poised and leading. 'My heart, prayers and deepest condolences are with the victims of the Manchester Attack and their loved ones,' she began. 'There is nothing I or anyone can do to take away the pain you are feeling or to make this better … I have been thinking of my fans, and of you all, non stop over the past week. The way you have handled all of this has been more inspiring and made me more proud than you'll ever know. The compassion, kindness, love, strength and oneness that you've shown one another this past week is the exact opposite of the heinous intentions it must take to pull off something as evil as what happened Monday.'

Ariana was more concerned with the victims and her other fans here and putting them in the centre of the story, than speaking of herself. 'We will not quit or operate in fear. We won't let this divide us. We won't let hate win.'

She continued: 'Our response to this violence must

be to come closer together, to help each other, to love more, to sing louder and to live more kindly and generously than we did before … I'll be returning to the incredibly brave city of Manchester to spend time with my fans and to have a benefit concert in honor of and to raise money for the victims and their families. I want to thank my fellow musicians and friends for reaching out to be a part of our expression of love for Manchester. I will have details to share with you as soon as everything is confirmed.'

This alone would have been an applaudable and mature reaction to such a tragedy. Yet this was just the beginning of what Ariana did. She was about to raise herself from her heartbreak – and raise all those who had been bowed by the atrocity. She decided she wanted to hold a concert back in Manchester, to remember the victims, heal the wounds and raise money for charity. Tickets for the event were made available on 1 June 2017 for £40. In keeping with the spirit of the show, they were sold with no booking fees. They sold out within six minutes of going on sale, though fans who were at the fateful concert of 22 May could apply to attend at no cost. Even with the concert merely announced, it felt like a healing process had begun. Once the concert actually began, that healing would continue. Ariana had been tested by this tragedy – and she was about to emerge a heroine.

CHAPTER ELEVEN

FROM THE ASHES

When Ariana flew back to the UK for her One Love Manchester Concert, she arrived with a certain level of esteem, but the stature with which she would leave the country was so much higher. For her fans, respect levels would rise even higher. Yet for the wider world, for those who had only vaguely heard of her before the terror attacks, Ariana's stature would soar.

She arrived at London's Stansted Airport two days before the event, with Joan at her side. Her father Ed and boyfriend Mac were also on the flight. She visited victims at Royal Manchester Children's Hospital. In photographs shared on social media, she was seen hugging youngsters. Her visit touched them deeply: it left one father in tears.

Peter Mann, whose daughter Jaden had been injured in the bombing, wrote on Facebook that Ariana's visit 'means more to us than all the amazing things people have done this week. when your daughter asks after her 2nd operation: Is Ariana OK? so happy she came i could burst! never seen Jaden so happy! even cried again myself.' Tasha Hough wrote: 'what a lovely girl Ariana Grande is.'

Ariana also knelt by the bed of Lily, aged eight, who had suffered a shrapnel wound and bruised lung in the attack. She told the youngster: 'I'm so proud of you. You are so strong. You are doing really well.' Lily's dad, Adam, said afterwards that the moment gave him goosebumps. Painting a picture with words, he added: 'Ariana lit the room up as soon as she walked in. She was absolutely fantastic. She had a big smile and was so enthusiastic. She knelt by Lily's bed and asked her lots of questions. She had so much time for her. Lily was bouncing off the walls. She was so excited. She is her biggest fan.'

'Lily was going pink and shy,' continued Adam, who himself suffered an abrasion to his right shoulder blade and a torn ligament in his left ankle at the show. 'It was such a positive thing for Ariana to do, after everything that happened last Monday. It was invaluable. She was so sincere. She brought a big Harrods teddy and some flowers for all the kids.'

With the visits paid, it was time for Ariana to prepare

for the benefit show. In a fateful time of trauma, there was to be one more twist. The night before the concert, there was a terror attack in London. A van left the road and struck a number of pedestrians on London Bridge, in the City of London. After the collision, the occupants of the van jumped out and fled to Borough Market in Southwark, a heavily populated bar and restaurant area, where they stabbed people at random. Eight people were killed and forty-eight injured. Ariana responded by tweeting in the early hours of Sunday: 'Praying for London'. Although the capital attack led to tighter security for the One Love show, it never threatened to cancel it. The show would go on.

And it would go on in front of a 50,000-crowd at Emirates Old Trafford cricket ground, with millions watching as it was broadcast live on BBC One. Coldplay, Katy Perry, Justin Bieber, Little Mix and Liam Gallagher were among those to appear. It was to be quite a night, and it began when Marcus Mumford introduced Take That. Gary Barlow said: 'Our thoughts are with everyone that's been affected by this, but right now, we want everyone to stand strong, look at the sky, sing loud and proud.' Robbie Williams added: 'Manchester, we're strong, we're strong, we're strong, we're still singing our songs, our songs.'

Will.i.am of the Black Eyed Peas told the crowd: 'We are here, we are together and we are one! We're showing love to Manchester and London right now – put your hands in the air in the name of love!' Before he left, he added: 'We love every single one of you. We would like to thank Ariana and show our appreciation for the mayor of London, the mayor of Manchester, the police force of Manchester, the police force in London and all these people who are fearless, who came for love, who will not be separated.'

Ariana told the crowd: 'One Love Manchester, let's go! We love you so much.' Thanking the crowd for 'coming together and for being so loving and strong', she spoke of her meeting with the mother of one of the young victims of the attack, Olivia Campbell, aged fifteen. 'I had the pleasure of meeting Olivia's mummy two days ago, I did my best not to cry and gave her a big hug. And she told me that Olivia wouldn't have wanted me to cry and then she told me that Olivia would have wanted to hear the hits. That being said we had to change everything and we wanted to fill it with love and energy. This evening has been so light and so filled with fun and love and bright energy, and I want to thank you for that.'

When Miley Cyrus joined her, Ariana said: 'Manchester, I want to thank you from the bottom of my heart for being here today. I love you so, so much. Thank you. I want to thank you so much for coming together and being so loving and strong and unified. I love you guys so much and I think that the kind of love and unity you're displaying is the medicine that the world needs right now.' Miley herself said: 'I am so honoured to be at this incredible event, surrounded by all of you amazing people and for me, the most important responsibility we have on this entire planet is to take care of one another and look what we're doing today.' Pointing to Ariana, Cyrus continued: 'She's a good role model for so many of you girls out here and I think she's proved that by putting this together and allowing all of us to be a part of it. I've always loved Manchester and not just today – it's always felt like a home away from home for me. So I'm happy to be back.'

Chris Martin of Coldplay took to the stage to huge cheers. He told Ariana: 'We all want to say thank you to you for being so strong and so wonderful. You've been singing a lot for us, so I think we in Britain want to sing for you.' He performed 'Fix You', 'Something Just Like This' and 'Viva La Vida'. Former Oasis frontman Liam Gallagher said: 'I want to dedicate this next song to the beautiful people who were killed and injured in the Manchester terror attack.'

As her managerial stablemate Justin Bieber arrived, he said: 'I'm not going to let go of hope, I'm not going to let go of love. I just want to take this moment to honour the people who were lost or that were taken. We love you so much. To the families, we love you so much.' He sang 'Love Yourself' and 'Cold Water'. Then there was the supersonic Katy Perry: 'We will not be silenced!' she told the crowd. 'I'm so honoured and humbled to be here tonight, to share and spread love. It's not easy to always choose love, is it? Especially in moments like these. It can be the most difficult thing to do. But love conquers fear and love conquers hate. And this love that you choose will give you strength and it's our greatest power.'

On and on came the stars. Little Mix's Jesy said: 'Thank you, Manchester, you've been incredible. It's been such an honour to be a part of tonight. Enjoy the rest of your evening, thank you, we love you.' As for One Direction's Irish heart-throb Niall Horan, he said: 'I've been lucky enough to have travelled all over the world and every time I come back to Manchester, I'm addicted to this place. You guys make everyone that comes from out of town feel so welcome and we really appreciate that, so when I saw you guys all rallying together last week, it was a sight to behold. It was incredible. We love you. We're with you.'

Pharrell Williams told Manchester to 'let the world hear your resilience'. He added: 'You know why I'm bowing? I'm bowing because despite all the things that have been going on in this place, I don't feel or smell or hear or see any fear. All we feel here tonight is love, resilience, positivity …' Meanwhile, Joan had joined fans in the crowd, telling them, 'Do not be afraid'. She had also shared supportive comments online, writing that her heart went out 'to all the victims', adding she stands with 'those who lost their lives, those injured, those recovering & all survivors of that night, along with the families & friends whose grief knows no bounds'.

The three-hour Manchester show was a triumph, watched by television viewers in more than fifty countries. It raised £2 million. Mike Adamson, chief executive of the British Red Cross, said: 'This benefit concert is a gesture of solidarity by Ariana Grande and the many other stars who have pledged their involvement.' No wonder the media was full of praise. In the *Daily Telegraph*, Neil McCormack wrote that the venue 'was awash with pink, with face paint, glitter and a menagerie of animal cars (cats, mice, bunny's and bea antennae)'. *Metro* called it 'a triumphant up yours to terrorism', while *Rolling Stone* said the event saw 'joy conquer fear'.

The Independent reprtcd that the event was the 'proper way to respond to hate', praising its 'pure spirit and determination'. It also noted that Ariana's 'much-awaited' performance brought 'the most deafening roar of the night'. *Forbes* magazine noted that the event 'required Grande to get back on stage and for many of those at her May 22 Arena concert to go back into a similar setting where the terror had occurred'. Here, it said, was why the concert mattered, because 'to be willing to so quickly do so was a strong testament that the human spirit will endure and that music's healing power remains undiminished'. Turning to Ariana's performance itself, *Forbes* continued: 'Credit goes to Ariana Grande: She didn't appear until an hour in, but it was her show from the start.'

Elsewhere, *NME* called it 'transformative', adding that 'the twenty-three-year-old's incredible composure had many in tears'. The BBC added that there were 'high emotions', saying that Ariana showed 'dignified emotion' as well as 'grit and willpower'. Perhaps most significantly, the BBC added: 'After tonight, she is idolized a little bit more by her fans, is higher in the estimation of those who had thought of her as a pop kitten, and is admired by those who only heard her name for the first time thirteen days ago.' *OK* magazine said, 'it'll undoubtedly go down in history as one of the most memorable and iconic musical event of all time' and 'a concert that never lost sight of the power of laughter and fun'.

All this emotional and sincere praise was wonderful for Ariana. Yet for one of those who praised her, the process involved an additional dimension: the eating of a huge serving of humble pie. The controversial and outspoken British journalist Piers Morgan had criticized Ariana in the wake of the bomb attack. Ever the Twitter opportunist, Morgan leapt into action when Katy Perry praised the Queen for visiting hospitalized victims of the blast. After the pop star tweeted: 'God bless The Queen and her kind heart', Piers replied. 'Agreed. Might have been nice if @ArianaGrande had stayed to do the same.'

Morgan's tweet immediately ignited the fiery reaction he was hoping for, with one Twitter user telling the broadcaster: 'Spectacularly ill thought out, that deserves a rethink, retraction and an apology.' However, the thick-skinned Morgan was having none of this. He wrote: 'If the Queen can visit the victims in hospital, so can the star they paid to see.'

As Ariana's fans bombarded him with disapproval, Morgan continued: 'I can 100 per cent guarantee you I would stay and visit those who had been killed or wounded watching me perform.' These words were somewhat academic, as a journalist in his fifties is unlikely to be giving a pop concert. However, after Ariana's One Love Manchester concert, he changed tune. Describing her as an 'admirable young woman' on Twitter, he added that she had put on a 'magnificent' show. He continued 'I thought Ariana Grande was wrong to fly off after #ManchesterAttack. But tonight she's putting on a fabulous show.' In the next of his series of tweets, he wrote: 'I'll say this too about @ArianaGrande – she has a cracking voice. By far the best vocal performance tonight ...'

As the concert came to an end, he concluded: 'I misjudged you, @ArianaGrande & I apologise. You're an admirable young woman & this is a magnificent night. Respect.' It is unlikely that Ariana craved Morgan's approval as much as he imagined she did, but nonetheless this was a high-profile victory for her. His previous criticism of her had travelled far and wide, thanks to the five million people who follow him on Twitter. Morgan is not famed for self-censure or self-awareness, so his admission that he 'misjudged' Ariana was a milestone at a sensitive time.

However, it was the praise of those who had managed to not publicly attack her in her darkest hour that felt the most sincere and nourishing. The city of Manchester recognized her work when its council announced that it will make her an honorary citizen of the city for her efforts in organizing the One Love benefit concert. 'This seems a fitting moment to update the way we recognize those who make noteworthy contributions to the life and success of our city,' council leader Sir Richard Leese told the BBC.

The benefit concert and associated Red Cross fund raised £10 million for victims of the attack. Ariana became the first patron of a charity set up for survivors and victims of the Manchester Arena attack. The We Love Manchester Emergency Fund has raised over £11.7 million to date, including the £3 million raised at the One Love Manchester concert. 'Ariana Grande exemplified Mancunian spirit', Councillor Sue Murphy, the chair of the charity, told the *Manchester Evening News*. 'Her fundraising concert raised millions for the appeal and buoyed all our spirits. We are grateful to her for agreeing to be patron of this charity, which seeks to help everyone who was affected by the tragedy.'

There was also a memorial concert for the victims held in New York. Staged at the Cutting Room nightclub, a group of Broadway performers and musical theatre artists joined forces to raise money for those affected. 'What happened at Ariana's concert was horrific. We – as artists, as New Yorkers, as humans – owe it to the people of Manchester to use our talents to support them with compassion and love and all the money we can possibly raise,' Alex Newell, who starred as Unique Adams in Fox's musical series *Glee*, told *Broadway World*. 'I could not think of a better way to spend a Sunday evening.'

For Ariana, honouring the victims of the attacks was not something she would do merely during her visit to the UK. It is an ongoing commitment. Following a July concert in Buenos Aires, she tweeted to her forty-eight million followers about Saffie Roussos, the youngest victim of the Manchester Arena bombing. 'Saffie, we're [thinking] of you baby', she wrote, alongside an emoji of a birthday cake.

However, the darker side of the story carries on, too. Could Ariana ever feel safe again? In July 2017, authorities in Costa Rica arrested a man suspected of threatening to stage an attack at one of her concerts. Prosecutors said in a statement that the suspect was a Colombian man of twenty-two, who made the threats online. The head investigator, Walter Espinoza, told local reporters that the threats were written in Arabic.

The suspect was held in a dawn raid on his flat in Tibás, near the capital San José. Police seized two mobile phones allegedly used to make the threats. Ariana would not be intimidated: the concert in the city of Alajuela, Costa Rica, went ahead as scheduled.

CHAPTER TWELVE

LOOKING TO THE FUTURE

For Ariana, her career will have new, more conventional, challenges in the years ahead. Part of the challenge will be updating her image to reflect her growing maturity, and that of her fans. At what stage will it be OK for her to become more 'adult' in her approach? 'I've taken baby steps in expressing my sexuality in my imagery,' she told *Cosmopolitan* in 2017. 'I'm all the way there now, but I'm also twenty-three, you know? I'm still figuring everything out, but it's tight to be at a point where I'm having fun with it, and I don't think that makes me any less of a role model. I think that it makes me honest!'

Speaking to the *Daily Telegraph* as far back as 2014, Ariana saw this problem coming. When she posted a photo of herself in a 'cute outfit with some kitty ears', giving the camera the middle-fingered salute on social media, she noticed varying results. 'My fans were like, "YES GIRL! OK!" A lot of my fans have grown up with me. But at the same time, a lot of people were like, "She's changing! What's happened to you?" I'm like, "It's just a pic, y'all. I'm still the same old me. I'm just posing in a cute way!" A lot of people go ape over one photo … But it's just a photo. I'm still the same person I've been since I was four years old. Literally. Obviously, I'm a mature adult. But I'm still the same girl. I'm still Ariana from Boca who loves musical theatre, who loves her family, who loves the beach, who loves animals.'

Speaking to *Time* magazine, Ariana said she 'absolutely' swears a lot. 'I'm Italian! I wish I could less,' she continued. As she spoke on, she pointed to what she saw as the confusion that arose as her career – and life – developed. 'I don't know why people are so shocked by me,' she said. 'I guess it's because of the character I played so long being such a goody two-shoes. But I also think that people have a misrepresentation of me as a person because I'm friendly and I like to meet people and I like to talk to people and make people laugh.' Ultimately, she concluded, being a role model is, 'Just being yourself And being unapologetically yourself, whatever that means.'

As her image and fan base becomes more adult, Ariana also finds herself as something of a gay icon. As well as her support for her brother Frankie and her disavowal of Catholic homophobia, there are several other reasons for her popularity among the gay male community. Some of these reasons are fairly obvious – for example, the backing track to 'Break Free' is just the sort of thing that gets gay nightclubs bouncing, and the accompanying video for the track – which includes a pink planet and a gay alien couple – also holds appeal.

But Ariana feels strongly about intolerance and homophobic attitudes and continues to speak out, palpably bristling as much as she did in the days when she moved from Catholicism to Kabbalah. 'It's outrageous to me when I see people hate on someone because of their sexuality,' she told *V* magazine. 'I hate the intolerance. I hate the judgment. I hate it so much. Most of my favorite people in my life are gay. It's something I'm super passionate about, because whenever I would see my friends get bullied, or my brother get hurt for his sexuality, I would become a raging lunatic.'

She also got brownie points from the gay community when she performed at New York Gay Pride in 2015. The event was particularly pumped because it came a matter of days after the US Supreme Court legalized gay marriage. 'Make some noise if you think the Supreme Court justices who voted against gay marriage should get their heads out of their f---ing asses and join the goddamn celebration!' she told the audience, to loud cheers.

'I mean, here's the thing: I wasn't raised in a household

where it was considered abnormal to be gay,' she said. 'So for me, to meet people who use the word "faggot" as an insult, with a derogatory meaning, I can't take it. I don't understand it. It's so foreign to me.' She continued, saying that when Frankie came out, 'it wasn't a big deal for my family'. She said that even her grandfather, 'who is like, super old-school, was like, "Good for you!"' She said that this familiarity and ease with homosexuality is something that has always been part of her life.

During an interview with the *Riff* magazine, Ariana was asked how she felt about her status as a gay icon. Rather than playing the moment down or brushing off the matter, Ariana showed her pride. 'That's my favorite thing anyone's ever said to me in my entire life,' she said. So when, in 2017, *Billboard* magazine named her the gay icon of the generation, arguing that she 'possesses so much style, swag, and support for the LGBTQ community' that the award was inevitable, one can only imagine her joy.

Her iconic status reaches wider than any individual community or identity group, though. As we have seen, she grew in the aftermath of the Manchester bombing. This has made her more than the cute young starlet she was prior to that tragic evening. She is now bigger and wiser – more mature. For many, she is the spokesperson for a generation.

Asked by the *New York Times* how she would avoid the pitfalls that befall many celebrities who found fame young, she gave an honest response when she replied: 'I don't know.' But she added: 'I have a really – actually, I do know – I have a really, really, really wonderfully supportive, perfectly, like, sane family. I feel like a lot of the teen celebrities who haven't been able to handle the fame and sort of messed up as a role model have not really had the full support of their family and that seems to be the root of the problem.'

Her fan base remains committed to their heroine: when she was overlooked for Artist of the Year at the 2017 MTV awards, with the title instead going to Ed Sheeran, the Arianators flooded Twitter with their outrage and disbelief. 'Ariana has done more than all of those artists and everyone knows it,' read one typical message. As the year rolled on, she also had to respond to a new trickle of suggestions of diva-like behaviour, after accusations that she was 'rude' and 'disrespectful' during her recent gig in South Korea. 'I cherish these shows and these very special times with you. I am enjoying every last moment and am eternally grateful for you,' she wrote on Twitter.

However, there is a real sense that, in the wake of the Manchester bombing and Ariana's response to it, the media now lack the appetite to chase any diva allegations against her. There might be smatterings of it here and there in the future, but it seems that Ariana has overcome that now: Ariana the hero is more part of their narrative, as they portray her in more mature terms. And if there is a moment in Ariana's life to take from this book, it should be the moment she stood on the stage at the One Love concert, healing the wounds of a heartbroken nation. She might be just a little over five feet in height, but here she stood tall, towering over any of the tittle-tattle that has swarmed around her in recent years.

But, as fans, we can hopefully expect more craziness and random moments from her. Asked what was the worst piece of advice she has ever been given, Ariana told Neon Limelight: 'Someone told me they only like me when I'm normal and that I should be more normal.' She went on: 'I guess the worst piece of advice I've ever been given was to be, like, not myself. If anyone ever tells you not to be yourself, that's the worst piece of advice you could ever be given.'

Be yourself: it's good advice for anyone to follow. As long as Ariana sticks to it herself, she will continue to enthrall the planet.

DISCOGRAPHY

ALBUMS

Yours Truly	Republic Records, 2013
My Everything	Republic Records, 2014
The Remix	Republic Records, 2015
Dangerous Woman	Republic Records, 2016

SINGLES

'Put Your Hearts Up'	Republic Records, 2011
'The Way'	Republic Records, 2013
'Baby I'	Republic Records, 2013
'Right There'	Republic Records, 2013
'Last Christmas'	Republic Records, 2013
'Love Is Everything'	Republic Records, 2013
'Snow in California'	Republic Records, 2013
'Santa Baby'	Republic Records, 2013
'Problem'	Republic Records, 2014
'Break Free'	Republic Records, 2014
'Bang Bang'	Lava/Republic Records, 2014

'Love Me Harder'	Republic Records, 2014
'Santa Tell Me'	Republic Records, 2014
'One Last Time'	Republic Records, 2014
'E Più Ti Penso'	Republic Records, 2015
'Focus'	Republic Records, 2015
'Dangerous Woman'	Republic Records, 2015
'Into You'	Republic Records, 2016
'Side to Side'	Republic Records, 2016
'Everyday'	Republic Records, 2017
'Beauty and the Beast'	Walt Disney, 2017

EPs

Christmas Kisses	Republic Records, 2013
Christmas & Chill	Republic Records, 2015

AWARDS

American Music Award: 2013, 2015, 2016

Bambi Award: 2014

iHeart Radio Music Award: 2014, 2015

MTV Video Music Award: 2014

People's Choice Award: 2014

Billboard Women in Music Award: 2014

MTV Europe Music Awards: 2013, 2014, 2016

MTV Italian Music Awards: 2016, 2017

MTV Millennial Awards: 2015, 2016

MTV Video Music Awards: 2014

MTV Video Music Awards Japan: 2014, 2015, 2016

Nickelodeon Kids' Choice Awards: 2014, 2015, 2016

People's Choice Awards: 2014

Teen Choice Awards: 2014, 2015, 2016

YouTube Music Awards: 2015

BIBLIOGRAPHY

Ariana Grande: The Book, Ariana Grande, ML Publishing, 2015

Birth Order, Linda Blair, Little, Brown, 2011

Justin Bieber: The Biography, Chas Newkey-Burden, Michael O'Mara Books, 2010

The Artist's Way, Julia Cameron, Penguin, 1992

PICTURE CREDITS

Page 1: Walter McBride / Corbis via Getty Images (both).

Page 2: Alberto E. Rodriguez / Getty Images (top); Andreas Branch / Patrick McMullan via Getty Images (bottom).

Page 3: Startraks Photo / REX / Shutterstock (top); John Lamparski / WireImage / Getty Images (bottom).

Page 4: Frazer Harrison / WireImage / Getty Images.

Page 5: Jason Merritt / WireImage / Getty Images.

Page 6: Bruce Glikas / FilmMagic / Getty Images (top); Startraks Photo / REX / Shutterstock (bottom).

Page 7: Bruce Glikas / FilmMagic / Getty Images (top left and bottom); Kristina Bumphrey / StarPix / REX / Shutterstock. (top right).

Page 8: Kevin Mazur / WireImage / Getty Images (top); Frazer Harrison / KCA2014 / Getty Images (bottom).

Page 9: Chloë Rice / Disney Parks via Getty Images (top); Jeff Kravitz / MTV1415 / FilmMagic / Getty Images (bottom).

Page 10: Kevin Mazur / MTV1415 / WireImage / Getty Images (top left); Gilbert Carrasquillo / FilmMagic / Getty Images (top right); Jun Sato / WireImage / Getty Images (bottom).

Page 11: Kevin Mazur / WireImage / Getty Images (top left); Chelsea Lauren / WireImage / Getty Images (top right); ABACA USA / PA Images (bottom).

Page 12: Frank Micelotta / REX / Shutterstock (top left); Startraks Photo / REX / Shutterstock (top right); Kento Nara / Geisler-Fotopress / DPA / PA Images (bottom).

Page 13: Jerome Domine / ABACA / PA Images (top); Matt Crossick / Empics Entertainment/ PA Images (bottom).

Page 14: Hubert Boesl / DPA / PA Images (top); Jeff Kravitz / AMA2016 / FilmMagic / Getty Images (bottom).

Page 15: Larry Marano / REX / Shutterstock.

Page 16: Kevin Mazur / One Love Manchester / Getty Images for One Love Manchester (top); Danny Lawson / AFP / Getty Images (bottom).

INDEX

A

Abedi, Salman Ramadan, 183, 188, 189
Aguilera, Christina, 52, 162
All That, 23, 54
AllMusic, 121, 172
American Idol, 52, 79
Annie, 28, 29, 35, 181
Ariana: The Book (Grande), 38, 215
A$AP Ferg, 119
AXS, 114
Azalea, Iggy, 104, 110, 111, 112

B

'Baby I', 93, 94, 98, 213
'Bang Bang', 123, 213
Barlow, Gary, 195
The Battery's Down, 49
'Be Alright', 166, 173, 178
'Be My Baby', 116, 123
'Best Mistake', 116, 123
BIA, 177
Bieber, Justin, 7, 64, 84, 88–90, 91, 100, 101–102, 135, 138,
143, 173–4, 195, 197
Bieber, Pattie, 64, 89
Big Sean, 94, 110, 111, 116, 141
Black Eyed Peas, 195
Braun, Scooter, 84–91, 96, 102, 112, 138, 142, 156, 173, 189
'Break Free', 114, 115, 116, 120, 122, 123, 172, 178, 207, 213
'Break Your Heart Right Back', 117, 123
Broadway in South Africa Concert, 50
Butera, Anthony (paternal grandfather), 14
Butera, Antonino (paternal great-great-grandfather), 14
Butera, Charles (paternal great-grandfather), 14
Butera, Florence (paternal grandmother), 14
Butera, Margherita (paternal great-great-grandmother), 14
Butera, Marie (paternal great-grandmother), 14

217

C

Cameron, Julia, 28, 216
Carey, Mariah, 36, 65, 78, 83,
  86, 97, 98, 100, 117, 121, 135,
  136–7, 139, 162, 166, 169
Carr, Alan, 37–8
Cashmere Cat, 116
Christmas & Chill, 214
Christmas Kisses, 102–3, 214
Clarkson, Kelly, 52, 78
Coldplay, 195, 197
Confessions on a Dance Floor, 74
Corbyn, Jeremy, 188
Corner, Lewis, 98, 114, 173
cyberbullying, 83, 181
Cyrus, Miley, 52, 54, 84, 97,
  138, 143, 155, 196, 197

D

'Dangerous Woman', 163, 165,
  178, 214
Dangerous Woman, 161–182, 213
Dion, Celine, 37, 139, 175
Disney, 52, 54, 121, 214
#donutgate, 151–9, 169, 174,
  181
Drake & Josh, 54

E

E, Mike, 131
E!, 136
E! News, 61, 139, 146
Eminem, 85
Empire, Kitty, 119, 180
Erlewine, Stephen Thomas,
  122, 172
Estefan, Gloria, 37, 38

E-Venture Kids, 39
'Everyday', 167, 170, 214

F

fandom, 14, 41, 58–60, 63, 64,
  78–9, 82, 93, 97, 99–102, 122,
  131–4, 138, 162, 163, 168, 180,
  209
  diva allegations, 131–4
  growing maturity, 205–6
  Manchester terror attack,
    184–8, 189, 191, 193–4,
    196–8, 200–201, 203
feminism, 146–7, 182
Fergie, 78
'Focus', 178, 214
'Forever Boy', 169, 178
Frankie (fragrance), 149
Franklin, Aretha, 89, 126
Future, 162, 167

G

Gallagher, Liam, 7, 195, 197
GarageBand, 43, 44
Garland, Judy, 9, 22, 34, 35
Geffen, David, 90, 91
Gillies, Elizabeth, 49, 50, 53, 59,
  63, 102
Goldstein, Wendy, 110, 112
Gomez, Selena, 14, 52, 171
Grande, Ariana, *211*
  agents, 52
  albums, *see by name*
  ancestry, 13–14, 206
  Bieber selfie, 101–2
  birth, 16
  boyfriends, 49–50, 59, 152

charitable causes, 36–7, 124, 175–6, 191, 199, 202

childhood, 9, 11–14, 16–20, 22, 32–41, 43–4, 47, 66, 80, 181, 206

confident nature, 45

copyright issues, 82

debut album. *see Yours Truly*

diva allegations, 130–142, 169, 181, 209

donutgate, 151–9

education, 17–18, 31, 48–9, 51–2

enterprising nature, 23

EPs, *see by name*

family Christmases, 13

family holidays, 37

fans *see* fandom

film career, 83

first public exposure, 23–5

first single, 75, 77–81, 99, 181

fragrances, 149

gay icon, 206–8

grandparents, 14, 16, 33, 36, 39, 101, 124, 134

growing maturity, 205–6, 209–10

horror movies, 11–13, 20, 21

hypoglycaemia, 20

ice-hockey incidents, 24

life coach, 137

Madonna collaboration, 75

managers, 22, 39, 84, 90, 91, 142, 156, 173–4. *see also* Braun, Scooter

Manchester concerts, 7–9, 183–4, 189, 190–91. *see also* Manchester terror attack; One Love Manchester

mimic skills, 36, 39, 174–5

musical tastes, 9, 22–3, 27, 33, 43–4, 45, 63, 78, 91–2, 120, 166

naming, 16

New York Gay Pride, 207

parents' divorce, 32–3

pop career, starts, 21, 63–5, 75, 77–83

promotional events, 82

public recognition, 58–9

record sales, 100, 124–5, 182

screen tests, 53

second album. *see My Everything*

self-confidence, 40, 164

sexism challenged, 143–8, 164–5

singles, *see by name*

sobriquets, 17, 28, 69

song-writing, 44–5, 49, 92, 110, 118, 181

spiritual beliefs, *see main entry*

stage career, 9, 27–32, 33–8, 45–6, 47–52, 52–5, 57, 65, 77, 176, 181

stand-up skills, 39

star sign, 19

strained family relations, 22

teenage years, 31, 38, 46, 48–9, 50, 52–3, 103, 181

third album. *see Dangerous Woman*

touring, 100–101, 162, 174,

176–9, 182
TV career, 39, 40–41, 52–8,
77, 80, 92, 101, 135, 155–6,
169, 181
Vevo channel, 81
White House performances,
126–7, 151
YouTube channel, 64–5, 77,
82, 155, 163
Grande, Edward ('Ed') (father),
14, 20, 24
birth, 15
career, 15
divorce, 32–3
education, 15–16
strained family relations, 22
wedding, 16
Grande, Frankie (half-brother),
157, 164
childhood, 17, 18
education, 17–18
fragrance, 149
sexuality, 67–8, 74, 206, 208
spiritual beliefs, 69, 74
stage career, 28, 34
Grande, Joan (mother), 11, 13,
20, 21, 24, 34, 47, 174
birth, 15
career, 15
dedication to children, 28
divorce, 32–3
first marriage, 17
Kids Who Care, 36
managerial skills, 39
Manchester terror attack,
184, 193, 198–9
wedding, 16

Grande-Butera, Ariana. see
Grande, Ariana
Gray, Macy, 162, 173
'Greedy', 167, 173, 178
Guetta, David, 114

H
Hairspray Live, 176
'Hands on Me', 118, 122
Heap, Imogen, 44, 181
Hicks, Gregory, 98
Hicks, Taylor, 52
Hilton, Paris, 72
Hinckley, David, 56
homophobia, 157, 179, 207–8
Horan, Niall, 198
Hough, Tasha, 194
Houston, Whitney, 22, 23, 65,
78, 126, 162, 175

I
'I Will Always Love You', 23, 175
IBI Designs, Inc., 15
iCarly, 54, 55, 56, 59
'Into You', 166, 178, 214
'Intro', 109

J
J, Jessie, 123, 139–140
Jackson, Michael, 88
'Just a Little Bit of Your Heart',
118, 123
Justice, Victoria, 53, 59

K
Kabbalah, 7, 69–72, 73–4, 75,
149, 163, 207

Kardashian, Kim, 143
KIIS-FM, 103
Kotecha, Savan, 110, 111, 112, 114, 162

L

LaBelle, Patti, 126
Lady Gaga, 139
Lambert, Dennis, 35–6, 36–7, 39–40
Lambert, Misha, 35, 36
'Last Christmas', 102, 213
'Let Me Love You', 167, 173, 178
Lewis, Leona, 119
Lily (fan), 194
Lipman, Monte, 65, 77, 99, 141
Lipshutz, Jason, 95, 120
Little Mix, 177, 195, 198
Lohan, Lindsay, 72
Lorde, 84
Lovato, Demi, 78, 154, 171
'Love is Everything', 102, 213
'Love Me Harder', 117, 123, 178, 214
Ludacris, 85, 88

M

McCormack, Neil, 199
McCurdy, Jennette, 59, 60, 61
McDermott, Maeve, 173
McIver, Elaine, 189
McLeod, Tom, 90
Madonna, 14, 23, 71, 72, 73, 74, 75, 139, 163, 175
Major Lazer, 125
Malik, Zayn, 143
Manchester memorial concerts,
7–9, 34, 203. *see also* One Love Manchester
Manchester terror attack, 7, 180, 183–190, 199, 202–3, 208, 209
Mann, Jaden, 194
Mann, Peter, 194
Marchione, Frankie (half-brother). *see* Grande, Frankie
Marchione, James (half-brother's half-brother), 18
Marchione, Victor (mother's first husband), 17, 18
Martin, Chris, 197
Martin, Max, 110, 112, 115, 116, 162
Miami Latin Boys, 37
Midler, Bette, 148
Mika, 96
Miller, Mac (boyfriend), 95, 189
Minaj, Nicki, 123, 147, 162, 166, 167
'Moonlight', 162, 163, 165, 170, 178
Moonlight by Ariana Grande (fragrance), 149
Morgan, Piers, 200–202
Mumford, Marcus, 195
mX, 135
My Everything, 107–127, 213

N

Nickelodeon, 23, 52, 54, 55, 57, 60, 63, 77, 101, 117, 119, 121, 122, 135, 169, 181, 215
93.3 FM, 82
96.1, 130
NME, 171, 200

O

Oasis, 197

Obama, Barack, 126

Obama, Michelle, 126

O'Connor, Jennifer ('Jen'), 131–4

O'Connor, Kelly, 132, 133–4

One Direction, 84, 118, 198

'One Last Time', 114, 120, 178, 180, 214

One Love Manchester, 193–202, 210

'Over the Rainbow', 7, 8–9, 22, 34, 35

P

Perry, Katy, 7, 95, 115, 138, 195, 197–8, 200

Phillips, Graham (boyfriend), 49

Pickhardt, Carl E., 33

'E Più Ti Penso', 214

'Problem', 110, 111, 113–114, 120, 122, 123, 172, 178, 181, 213

'Put Your Hearts Up', 78–81, 181, 213

R

Raising Malawi Foundation, 175–6

The Remix, 213

Republic Records, 65, 77, 91, 99, 100, 110, 112, 123, 141, 213, 214

'Right There', 94, 126, 213

Roussos, Saffie, 189, 203

Ruthie (Kabbalah teacher), 73

S

Sam & Cat, 59–63, 101, 135, 181

Samuels, Harmony, 95, 109

'Santa Baby', 102, 213

Sarah (fan), 185

Sarandon, Susan, 158

Saturday Night Live, 39, 155, 156, 174

SB Projects, 87

scandals, celebrity, 60, 127, 129–142, 149, 151, 169, 174, 181, 209

Seacrest, Ryan, 79, 82, 164

sexism, 143–8, 164

Sheeran, Ed, 44

'Side to Side', 166–7, 178, 214

Simone, Nina, 173

'Snow in California', 102, 213

So So Def Recordings, 86, 87

'Sometimes', 167–8, 178

Spears, Britney, 14, 52, 72, 87, 93, 115, 138, 174–5

spiritual beliefs, 8, 21, 67–72, 73–4, 75, 149, 158, 163, 186, 207

Sputnik Music, 171

'The Star-Spangled Banner', 40–41

Stefani, Gwen, 14

Styles, Harry, 118

Sweet Like Candy (fragrance), 149

Swift, Taylor, 146

T

Take That, 7, 195

'Tattooed Heart', 94, 126

terror attacks, 180, 183–190, 195, 203–4 *see also* Manchester terror attack

'Thinking Bout You', 170, 179

13, 46, 47, 48, 49, 50, 52, 53, 181

Timberlake, Justin, 52

'Tomorrow', 29, 30

The Tonight Show, 32, 174

'Touch It', 169, 178

Trump, Donald, 157, 179

U

Usher, 86

V

Victorious, 49, 53–4, 55–9, 63, 78, 92, 102, 181

Viscomi, Jordan (boyfriend), 59

The Voice, 139, 176

W

Walk, Charlie, 99, 100, 112–113

Wanted, 96

Waters, John, 176

'The Way', 81–3, 94, 181, 213

Wayne, Lil, 162, 167

Weeknd, 118

West 42nd Street, 47

West, Kanye, 87

White House, 126–7, 151, 179

'Why Try', 114, 120, 123

will.i.am, 195–6

Williams, Pharrell, 198

Williams, Robbie, 195

Winehouse, Amy, 94

The Wizard of Oz, 9, 22, 34–5, 181

Wonder, Stevie, 176

X

X, 125

The X Factor, 119

x-rated lyrics, 117, 167

Y

Y-100 Miami, 82

Ying Yang Twins, 112

Yours Truly, 81, 84, 91–105, 108, 109, 121, 125, 161, 167, 213

Z

Zach Sang and the Gang, 81

Zedd (producer), 115, 116

Zohar, 69–71, 74

Z100, 82

Zulu, Chaka, 88